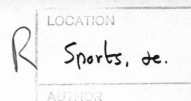

D1339238

APARTHEID
THE REAL HURDLE
Sport in South Africa & the International Boycott

by

Sam Ramsamy

International Defence and Aid Fund for Southern Africa
104 Newgate Street London EC1

1982

The International Defence and Aid Fund for South Africa is a humanitarian organisation which has worked consistently for peaceful and constructive solutions to the problems created by racial oppression in South Africa.

It sprang from Christian and humanist opposition to the evils and injustices of apartheid in South Africa. It is dedicated to the achievement of free, democratic, non-racial societies throughout Southern Africa.

The objects of the Fund are:—

(i) to aid, defend and rehabilitate the victims of unjust legislation and oppressive and arbitrary procedures,

(ii) to support their families and dependents,

(iii) to keep the conscience of the world alive to the issues at stake.

In accordance with these three objects, the Fund distributes its humanitarian aid to the victims of racial injustice without any discrimination on the grounds of race, colour, religious or political affiliation. The only criterion is that of genuine need.

For many years, under clause (iii) of its objects, The Fund has run a comprehensive information service on affairs in Southern Africa. This includes visual documentation. It produces a regular news bulletin 'FOCUS' on Political Repression in Southern Africa, and publishes pamphlets and books on all aspects of life in Southern Africa.

The fund prides itself on the strict accuracy of all its information.

ISBN No. 0 904759 50 4

Printed in England by Shadowdean Ltd. London

Contents

Introduction

In 1976, the year of the Montreal Olympics, the International Defence and Aid Fund, published *Race against Race–South Africa's "Multinational" Sports Fraud* (by Joan Brickhill, July 1976). *Apartheid–The Real Hurdle* is intended to update and expand upon that publication, in the light not only of the changes in the administration, promotion, control and general appearance of South African sport, but also of the important developments that have taken place—and the successes that have been won—in the international sports boycott of apartheid. It is hoped that this will prove useful not only to sportsmen and women, but to those who, throughout the international community, are anxious to see a non-racial, democratic and free South Africa take its place once again on the sports fields of the world.

Sport has always played a major role in propagating apartheid internationally. Internally the South African government has used international acceptance of its sports teams as a way of boosting white morale. Through the elevation of sport to a 'sacred cow' status by supporters and defenders of South Africa, apartheid itself has achieved sanctity. The cliche that sport and politics should be separated, furthermore, has been used by the apartheid regime and its supporters to retain South Africa's place in international sport.

Since 1966 the Supreme Council for Sport in South Africa, with the help of Socialist, Asian, Caribbean and some South American countries, has campaigned vigorously for the isolation of South African sport. This campaign has been largely effective because the rules of the International Olympic Committee and many international sports federations demand that if, by a majority decision, a country is expelled, the decision is binding on all members of the said federation. This has resulted in countries which previously supported South Africa having to sever their relations.

In all the major team sports—rugby being the notable exception—South Africa has been isolated relatively successfully. It has been expelled or suspended from international competitions in almost all the sports disciplines and many governments have discouraged links with apartheid sport.

However, in sports which have a stronger western influence or control it has proved much harder to isolate South Africa. In this respect it is worth noting that the western countries which support South Africa economically and politically are also those which wish to have sports exchanges with apartheid. South Africa still enjoys a fair degree of international participation in tennis, archery, golf, professional boxing, squash, yachting and equestrian sport, simply because these disciplines are controlled by western countries. In rugby the western countries, with the exception of Australia, give the apartheid regime, as they have always done, total support. The motivation for retaining South Africa's membership would seem to be purely political. The links are amply illustrated by statements made by the former Prime Minister of white South Africa:

'In cases where we have been kicked out, it has not, except in isolated instances, been the western countries which took the initiative or which were in favour of it.'

'Western countries tell us that they have no objection to playing against us, or to us attending this or that sports meeting of theirs.'[1]

As South Africa was expelled or suspended from various codes of sport the whites began to realise for the first time that they were being denied opportunities to display their talents. In an attempt to regain international credibility the white South African authorities have used various ploys and concessions to give the impression that sports relations within the country are being 'normalised'. The apartheid regime now maintains that all its national teams are elected on merit on a non-racial basis.

The socio-political system within South Africa demands the total separation of the races. The people are designated by law to live in their respective group areas, children are directed to separate schools and black school children—the raw material from which future black sportsmen and women are made—are forced to accept inferior and unequal facilities. It is in reality impossible to conceive of a completely non-racial sports system in a country which in these much more fundamental respects treats more than 80 per cent of the population differently on the grounds of race and colour. Merit selection emanating out of such a system has little or no meaning as it will tend to prove how mediocre the performances of black sportspeople are—the very theory that the white racist regime is propagating internationally.

The racial structure of South African society has led to the formation of several national bodies for the control of each particular sport.

This makes South Africa unique. Nowhere else in the world are sports facilities built specifically for the exclusive use of one particular racial group. Nowhere else in the world are there statutory demarcations which restrict the use of facilities exclusively to one racial group within the population.

Despite all the South African government's propaganda claims that non-racial sport is now permitted the laws that directly and indirectly affect the playing of mixed sport are still entrenched in South Africa's statute books. Blacks must still undergo the humiliation of being treated like second class citizens beyond the mandate of officially sanctioned *bona fide* sports fixtures for which honorary white status is conferred upon them. These few sports concessions are offered to blacks in order to re-open the way for South Africa's participation in international sport.

It is not possible to play genuine non-racial sport while the permit system, whether it is called 'consultation', 'co-operation' or anything else, continues to regulate and control the degree of mixing on the sports field. The changes effected in South African sport can only be cosmetic, and never fundamental, so long as they merely involve amending the laws of apartheid. Only the complete revocation of the laws of apartheid can see the establishment of non-racialism in sport.

In its attempts to confuse and mislead international opinion white South Africa has introduced a plethora of terms to define its sports structure. This book attempts to explain the various definitions but it must be emphasised that the term 'multi-racial sport' has a different connotation in South Africa from that in other parts of the world. The South African definition refers to the bringing together of the various racial groups for specific sports events where individuals are identified according to the racial label which apartheid attaches to each and every person in South Africa. Sports participation thereby becomes 'inter-racial' or 'multi-racial' rather than non-racial.

Inside South Africa, blacks wish to be treated as human beings every day of the week and not to be grudgingly accepted for a mixed match on a Saturday afternoon and then told to return to the humiliation of being second class citizens until the next sports fixture. Tony Ward, an Irish rugby player who toured South Africa in 1980 with the Lions but refused in 1981 to return with the Irish rugby team, aptly summarised the situation:

'But at the end of the day you and I play a game and then we go to the bar for a pint. If you are black in South Africa that is not possible. I go to the bar and you go to your township or wherever . . . and I'm alone in the bar with my pint. That's neither rugby, sporting nor moral.'[2]

1. History—Internal Resistance

The struggle for recognition by black sportsmen and women

Modern European sport was first introduced into South Africa during the nineteenth century by the British army and early British settlers. Extra leisure time at the disposal of the settlers, combined with the excellent climate for outdoor activities, inspired them to form clubs and associations in the various sporting codes. Afrikaners soon joined the British settlers. This was later followed by the formation of sports bodies by black groups. As black groups were socially and residentially separated from the whites, they belonged to separate associations.

White sports bodies, although constitutionally barring blacks from membership, never had racial labels for their clubs or associations; it was always 'Durban Surf Club', 'Natal Football Association', 'Transvaal Cricket Union', etc. On the other hand, black clubs and associations, although constitutionally not barring membership from other racial groups, had names such as 'Durban Indian Golf Club', 'Transvaal African Football Association', 'Natal Coloureds Hockey Association', etc. No doubt this was due to the forcible separation of the different black racial groups socially and residentially. However, the establishment of 'inter-racial sports boards' ensured mingling and competition between the various black groups. The white sports organisations refused to affiliate to these inter-race sports boards.

Between 1895 and 1910 most of the whites-only organisations, such as the South African Cricket Association, the South African Amateur Athletic Association and the South African Olympic Games Association, were admitted to international and/or British Empire sports federations. This gave them a 'passport' to compete with or against national teams of other countries for international honours.

Although white organisations held national open championships (in golf, athletics, swimming, etc.) which were recognised by the international and British Empire sports associations, blacks were always barred from taking part. Blacks were left out of South Africa's national teams even after they had gone abroad at tremendous expense and sacrifice and, in many cases, proved their competence.

It must be realised that at that stage the Nationalist South African government (elected in 1948) had not yet come to power with its policy of apartheid. Racial discrimination in sport was only a social practice at the time. Indeed, it was not until the Nationalist Party had been in power for a number of years that particular laws (notably the Group Areas Act) began to be used by the South African government for purposes of prohibiting and suppressing mixed sport. (Even then they did not always succeed—*see Ch. 2*).

By 1945 most of South Africa's all-white sports federations had not only established firm links with national sports organisations of other countries, but had also managed to get into executive positions in many international federations. Meanwhile, in South Africa, the whites continued to refuse blacks a place in their national teams, irrespective of the ability of black sportsmen and women. Black sportsmen and women, and sports administrators, frustrated by the uncompromising attitude of whites, appealed to the international and Commonwealth Games associations for help.

They were not successful in these early years. Many national and international associations were unsympathetic to their pleas. For instance, Oscar State, the then Secretary of the British Amateur Weightlifters' Association and until recently active in international weightlifting, replied to an appeal by black sportsmen on 13 May 1946 as follows:

'Please pardon my delay in replying to your letter but I had to wait until I placed the matter before our Central Council. They considered your request with sympathy but it is with regret that I have to inform you that we cannot bring any pressure on the South African Weightlifting Federation to force them to recognise you. Their rules, as with all national sporting associations in South Africa, will not permit of mixed contests between white and Coloured athletes.

This is also a condition of the South African Olympic Council. Therefore, no Coloured man could be chosen to represent South Africa in the international contests. For these reasons we cannot support your claim against the South African Weightlifting Federation.'

The only alternative left to black South Africans to gain international recognition was to go abroad. Because of prohibitive cost, only a handful could leave South Africa.

In 1946, several black South African boxers managed to campaign in Britain. Seaman Chetty, one of the early arrivals, was rated sixth contender for the British Empire Bantamweight title. Jake Ntuli, who sparred regularly with Vic Toweel, the white boxer who was then South African World Bantamweight Boxing Champion, arrived in England in 1952. Ntuli, at one sparring session, knocked Toweel out of the ring. In 1953, Ntuli knocked out Gardiner of England to become the British Empire Flyweight Boxing Champion. At the height of his career he was unanimously hailed by internationally recognised boxing scribes as the best flyweight boxer in the world. Only Pascuel Perez's (of Argentina) delaying tactics in arranging a World Championship fight prevented him from becoming a world champion. The number one contender for the world title was, in the eyes of the white-controlled South African Boxing Board of Control, however, not good enough to become a South African champion.

Davis Samaai played tennis at Wimbledon, but was not considered good enough to enter open tournaments in South Africa. In 1968 and 1969 the black South African Lawn Tennis Union sent some of its promising players to participate in European tournaments. In 1968, Jasmat Dhiraj and Herman Abrahams won the North of England Men's Doubles Championship and in 1969 Dhiraj won the South of England Singles Championship. Dhiraj and Miss Paddy Orchards also won the Mixed Doubles Championships in that year. In 1968 Dhiraj and Abrahams qualified for the Wimbledon Tennis Championships.

In 1971 a private match was arranged between Dhiraj and Cliff Drysdale, a white South African, who at the time was one of the top seeds in world tennis. Drysdale won the best of the three sets match 6-4 and 7-5. Immediately after the match, Drysdale publicly announced that Dhiraj was good enough to take part in the South African Open Tennis Championships. But this was never accepted by the white Union.

Although Ron Elland by far exceeded the total weight lifted by any white South African weightlifter in his division, he was told that he could not represent South Africa. He then left for England. He qualified to lift for Britain and then later became a member of the 1948 British Olympic Team.

For identical reasons, the weightlifter Precious McKenzie left South Africa for England in 1964. Since then he has taken part in three Olympic Games.

The late Sewsunker Papwa Sewgolam won the Dutch Open Golf Championship in 1959 and 1960. In 1963, after extensive world pressure, Sewgolam was allowed to compete in the South African Golf Championships and finished runner-up, but was not even considered for South Africa's Canada Cup Team.

Albert Johannson played football for the famous British Leeds United. He was the first black person to play in a F.A. Cup Final in Britain. He had no chance to represent South Africa.

Basil D'Oliveira, a Coloured South African, was a regular member of the MCC Cricket Team for several years. In 1962 he was selected to represent the World Cricket Team; yet he was not 'eligible' for the South African side.

These are only a few of the black South Africans who managed to leave South Africa to compete overseas and win international honours. But what about the thousands who could not afford to do so?

While not condoning their actions, it may be recorded that some black South Africans of fairer skin had tried to get into South African teams by 'playing white'.

Smilee Moosa (alias Williams), a black South African, managed to get into the all-white Berea Park Football Club as a player. Berea Park played in the all-white National Football League of the white Football Association of South Africa. Eventually Moosa's identity was exposed; he was immediately

11

expelled from the club of which he had been a first team player for months.

Until 1970, Topham, a Coloured South African living in Johannesburg's black township of Coronationville, was enrolled in a white judo club. Keeping his identity secret he managed to qualify to represent South Africa abroad. No one suspected he was black until the presentation of the South African Springbok Colours. He had to produce his identity card and was exposed. Although he represented South Africa later on several occasions he was never, because he was black, awarded Springbok Colours.

The South African Sports Association (SASA)

By the 1950s, black sports organisations had been organised into federations. Nevertheless, they were still excluded from world games because white sporting organisations, which had already forged international affiliations, were not prepared to accept black members. Without exception, international sports federations follow a policy of only recognising one affiliate from each country. South Africa's sporting policy was by now inextricably bound up with the Nationalist government's political and social policy; and as there was little hope that white sporting organisations would adopt a more liberal outlook towards blacks, black sports organisations took the initiative to campaign for recognition both at home and abroad.

In 1955 the Committee for International Recognition was formed in Durban. Its aim was to get South African non-racial bodies affiliated to international sports federations. In 1956 it succeeded in getting the South African Table Tennis Board of Control affiliated to the International Table Tennis Federation. The white association was expelled from the latter because it practised racial discrimination.

The South African Sports Association (SASA) was formed in 1958 as a counter to the white Olympic and Empire Games Association. Its main objective was to fight for the complete elimination of racial discrimination in sport in South Africa. SASA sent a memorandum to the International Olympic Committee in Rome in 1959 which stated, *inter alia:*

> 'It is the contention of non-racial sporting bodies that it is the right of all sportsmen of a country to be considered on merit for selection in teams representing their country, and that the South African national bodies, by excluding the non-whites of the country, have flouted the canons of sportsmanship. It must be noted that the non-whites have no desire to see their white compatriots excluded, and they insist that only merit be the criterion, without consideration of extraneous issues, such as colour, race or creed'.

The South African Non-Racial Olympic Committee (SAN-ROC)

SASA failed in its attempts to win the support of the Olympic Committee. Unable to win recognition or to persuade white sports associations to abandon their 'whites only' policy, and after the frustrating attempts by black sportsmen to become members of the South African Olympic and Commonwealth Games Association, SASA, together with a number of black sportsmen and sports administrators, formed the South African Non-Racial Olympic Committee (SAN-ROC) on 13 January 1963, in Johannesburg. Since then SAN-ROC has campaigned at international sports congresses for the rights of South Africa's black sportsmen and women and demanded exclusive recognition for non-racial teams from South Africa.

The reconstitution of black bodies into non-racial organisations

'Our goal is complete non-racial swimming—at every level in the country—administered by a single, truly non-racial swimming organisation; not the useless, ineffective and misleading body like the Amateur Aquatics Federation of South Africa.'[1]

Until 1962 black sports organisations were loosely held together by so-called 'Inter-Race Sports Boards' which linked the different sections of the black community (African, Asian and Coloured) and provided for inter-racial competitions at regional and national levels. Of all the inter-race boards, the South African Soccer Federation was by far the strongest as regards playing strength and spectator appeal. In 1962, the Federation, realising that several racial clashes had resulted from the artificial compartmentalisation of black soccer players and fans, decided to go completely 'non-racial' at all levels. When the other inter-race boards followed suit, apartheid legislation became operative. White sports officials immediately realised that the move was a direct threat to segregated sport and co-operated with the police and Government to crush or fragment non-racial sport.

Despite major problems (including police intimidation and the closure of sports grounds), black sportsmen and women persevered with the principle of non-racialism. Non-racial sport began to attract a fair degree of popularity among black South Africans. They nevertheless frequently found it impossible to put the principle into practice due to legal impediments and other obstruction.

The South African Council on Sport (SACOS)*

Despondent and impatient at the lack of progress towards non-racial sport in South Africa, representatives of a number of national sports organisations gathered in Durban for a conference in September 1970.

The conference resolved to tackle a number of problems confronting sport. Among the main resolutions were:

(a) To strive for a complete, non-racial sports structure (from school level upwards);

(b) To express strong opposition and expose discrimination in sports and sports sponsorship;

(c) To seek facilities that were deserving of all irrespective of colour;

* At its Extra-Ordinary Executive Meeting held in Yaounde, Cameroon on 24 and 25 January 1977, the Supreme Council for Sport in Africa granted observer status to SACOS. This decision was ratified at the General Assembly of the Supreme Council for Sport in Africa held in Rabat, Morocco in November 1977.

and
(d)   to form a national, non-racial sports organisation.

A subsequent meeting of this conference held in 1973 made a detailed study of racialism in sport and the failure of white bodies to show a genuine desire to resolve the situation. At this later conference the South African Council on Sport (SACOS) was born.

SACOS is now a serious threat to the white Olympic Council and it has geared itself to become a real force in South Africa.

In February 1978, SACOS clearly spelt out its demands:

'We know we have time on our side but we need all the allies we can get, especially at the international level. The cards are in our hands, and how we play them will be of great importance for the future development of this country, not only in the sports arena but beyond that. If at this juncture we accept concessions grudgingly given, the reluctant suggestions of amalgamation from our new-found fair-weather friends, and lose sight of our non-racial objectives, we may as well temporarily halt the march towards truly non-racial sports in a truly democratic society. The halt must be a temporary one as the process cannot be stopped. But we can contribute to its being prolonged unless we identify ourselves fully with the forces of progress. We say that what we are offered is not enough. We demand all rights for all citizens of this country whether they are sportsmen or not. We demand the right to have truly non-racial sport, whether soccer or cricket or tennis, at the spectator, player and administrative levels. We demand the right to be selected on merit at all levels. We demand that these rights not only be but be *seen* to be. When we speak in this manner then, and then only, will we be contributing positively towards the creation of a climate in which the goal of r on-racial sport in a non-racial society can be achieved. And we feel that any assistance, whether internal or external, whether national or international that will help to isolate racialism and bigotry in sport, will make an active contribution towards the achieving of such goals.'[2]

SACOS has 17 national sports disciplines affiliated to it and they have resolved unanimously:

'SACOS in a declaration of its solidarity with the Supreme Council for Sport in Africa hereby rejects all forms of racialism in sport and accepts a complete moratorium on all sports tours to and from South Africa until all the trappings of apartheid have been removed from South African sport.'

Despite government and official sabotage, police intimidation and prosecutions, SACOS has thus far managed to survive. Some of its affiliates have gained international respect for their uncompromising stand against segregated sport. White South Africa regards SACOS and its affiliates as 'polically motivated' and 'a nuisance'.

Recently a number of white sports administrators, together with their black allies, have been active in trying to infiltrate some non-racial organisations and have managed to induce a few of their officials to accept certain compromises. In a resolution adopted on 29 December 1977 SACOS agreed to expel any member who practiced 'double standards' in non-racial sport.

All SACOS affiliates have accepted this resolution which, very simply, means that a sportsman/woman belonging to an affiliate of SACOS in one code of sport (e.g. football) cannot belong to a racial unit in another code of sport (e.g. athletics). Such a sportsman or woman is barred from all activities of SACOS on the grounds that his/her action amounts to double standards.

SACOS hopes, through such action, to rid its membership of corrupt and self-seeking persons. More and more blacks are now realising the value of such a resolution and the students, in particular, are beginning to take the lead.

To date white sportsmen and women inside South Africa have, by and large, remained aloof from the growing campaign of resistance to apartheid sport. There has not been a single case of a white organisation defying the government's sports policy. Those few white individuals who, in collaboration with black organisations, have made their commitment to non-racial sport public through various acts of defiance, have become social outcasts from the white community.

Table: National sports disciplines affiliated to SACOS
    Amateur Swimming Association of South Africa
    South African Amateur Athletic Board
    South African Amateur Weightlifting and Body Building Federation
    South African Billiards and Snooker Control Board
    South African Baseball Federation
    South African Cricket Board
    South African Cycling Board
    South African Darts Board of Control
    South African Hockey Board
    South African Non-Racial Amateur Golf Association
    South African Netball Association
    South African Rugby Union
    South African Soccer Federation
    South African Softball Federation
    South African Table Tennis Board
    South African Women's Hockey Board
    Tennis Association of South Africa

Schools
    South African Primary Schools Sports Association
    South African Senior Schools Sports Association

Document I: Policy Statement of the South African Council on Sport

'Why we reject the present sports structure'
'The future of the government's sports policy stands at the crossroads of indecision and uncertainty today. There have been protestations from the state that racism does not exist in sports any more. And there have been promises of changes for a better sports future. But, better for whom, we ask? For the architects of racialism and their coterie who have been rebuffed by the international community? Or for the majority of our people who have become used to the tricks of racial chameleon?

The non-racial sports movement has reflected these "changes", for it knows that they are only cosmetic. Whatever these changes are they certainly have not filtered into the roots of injustice in this country. And even if the face of the sports structure ultimately changes into a more seductive ploy to hoodwink those in our community who are naive about manipulated change, it cannot hide the scars of sustained injustice over our lives. For, the lives of the majority of our people in the shackled corners of our land throb daily with the pain and misery of social deprivation. And they know that the planting of the seeds of love for justice and truth continues to yield more chaff than grain. They cannot be fooled by meaningless concessions while the skeleton in the apartheid cupboard continues to rattle with years of injustice.

When the non-racial sports movement against racialism in sports was born, it also had visions of a freedom in all aspects of our lives. While its campaign was aimed primarily at drawing attention to the unjust sports in the country, and fighting for the eradication of the apartheid virus that has contaminated the sports fields, it also recognised that sport as a social phenomenon is just a microcosm of society. Therefore, any changes in this structure would be irrelevant if the society as a whole did not undergo a racial transformation for the better. It was the recognition of this fact that led to a determination to expose the fraudulent nature of concessions in sports for as long as the total society continued to labour under the injustices of white supremacy. And it is this perspective that is captured in our contention that there can be no normal sports in an abnormal society. This is why clever manoeuvres by the architects of apartheid to manipulate changes in just one segment of our lives is rejected outright by non-racialists.

Destroyed by legislation
To understand the present sports structure in its proper context, and our reasons for rejecting it, we need to go back a little into the history of sports in the country. With the coming of the nationalist government into power, whatever precious freedom of association that may have existed was destroyed by legislation, and separatism was enforced through various acts of parliament. This was merely an extention and confirmation by legislation of the deep rooted prejudices and injustices of the whites. While legislation entrenched the avowed rejection of the rights of the blacks, the more abhorrent result was the attempt to destroy the bridges of friendship that were being forged by the various black race groups. The whites in power were not content with keeping the choice fruits of our people's labour to themselves, but also interfered with the right of the deprived people to socialise across the borders of race. But while physical separation through the Group Areas Act was ruthlessly perpetuated, the spirit of non-racialism, and relating with people as one human being to another, could not be destroyed. Black sportspersons came together frequently in spite of hostilities of law. More laws were made, but faith in the non-racial

cause was beginning to stir the coming winds of change.

It was not long before the international sporting fraternity began taking a peek into the mirror of South African society. What they saw there disgusted them, and the road towards exposing and isolating a pariah among nations took its course.

The drum beats of hope that have echoed through an oppressed nation once more began heralding another road to freedom. White South Africa pretended at first not to hear them. But increasing isolation changed escapist dreams into uneasy nightmares. Something had to be done to counteract these threats and to placate the discomfort of western friends. There were desperate attempts to sweep the muck of apartheid under the carpet, but the sovereignty of the nation and the herrenvolk way of life had to be protected at all costs.

Multi-national sports were then reintroduced, and friendship engineered with renegades from the non-racial movement. Impassioned campaigns, backed by financial perks from major business, were launched in the corridors of overseas governments. "Sport in South Africa is normal", is the cry today. There are some who have fallen for the bluff and continue to aid and abet the government in its efforts to seek acceptance internationally and strangle the non-racial movement.

But the struggle of non-racialism continues to thwart these cosmetic changes. Non-racial sportspersons have consistently rejected the present sports structure.

Why?

Because there is a truth to life in this country that cannot be hidden. The drum beats for freedom that have echoed through the ages continue to sound, notwithstanding the cosmetic changes promoted by those in power. For, no modern myth, nor selective changes in the sports structure, nor mirror-dressing, can erase the scars of oppression that riddle the self-same societal mirror. Because state attempt at "normal" mixing in the sports field, cannot remove the tragic reflection of starving mouths and embittered souls. Because there is neither logic nor morality in the prospect of momentary justice and non-racialism on the sports field on the one hand, and the inevitable return to the ghettoes and legislatively separated areas on the other. Because there is equally no morality in showing the world how "non-racial" the government is in sports, while the educational, welfare, industrial, social, and political pinnacles of society are racially fettered.

There is an inter-dependence between a society and its sporting system. Sport is a by-product of society. It reflects the spiritual wealth of a society. Or it reflects its political decay. Those who attempt to see meaningful changes in the sports structure cannot expect to see much change for as long as the larger society remains unchanged. In South Africa, laws such as the Group Areas Act and Liquor Act that govern our daily lives, have also been chiefly responsible for the present racial sports structure. The removal of these laws from the sports arena cannot make society free. It is because of this act that the recommendation of the Human Sciences Research Council (HSRC) for the removal of "all hurtful discrimination" in sports cannot be accepted. The shadow of legislated prejudice will still haunt us when we return from the cricket match and make us virtual prisoners in our own country.

It is an example of the peculiarity of life here that recommendations like those of the Human Sciences Research Council try to project the impression that freedom can exist on the sports field while repression rules everywhere else. There is a further fundamental consideration that needs to be understood. It is that state policy has ensured that, wherever blacks live, they have to contend with the most deplorable sports facilities, or even no facilities. And major enterprises that thrive on black labour offer little in return. Equally significant is the fact that, while the government is bent on resuming international sports ties, and while it attempts to out-manoeuvre the non-racial campaign, there are children in South Africa who languish in the dark recesses of apartheid society, knowing little of a pleasure called participatory sports; experiencing little of the opportunities reserved for the children of the privileged; but living the dread of malnutrition and social and psychological deprivation from conception to the struggle for manhood.

It is the pulse of common brotherhood that deems that we cannot accept the present sports structure while law and ideology militate daily against the quest for decency and justice. And it is the greater morality that transcends the sports struggle that dictates that, for as long as the stifled sobs and tear-stained cheeks of our children haunt the darkness of dejected corners in dignified pride, for so long must those who express a commitment to the cause of non-racialism, in sports and society, refuse to succumb to cosmetic changes. The sum total of South African society clearly underlines the truth that South Africa's sports structure has not changed. Only the nuances have. Can any acceptance of it be compatible with the cause we espouse?'

(Statement by South African Council on Sport (SACOS), first published in Souvenir Brochure of the Natal Council of Sport 13.12.80).

2. The Legal Basis of Apartheid Sport

There is no law or legal clause in South Africa which specifically prohibits mixed sport. However laws which are indirectly linked with certain activities which include sport, together with government policy generally, militate against the free playing of mixed race sport.

In the early days of international sport it was generally accepted by all South Africans that only whites were eligible to represent South African national teams. Only when blacks began to challenge the exclusive white nature of South African sport did white sports administrators and government officials seek out the fine print in the apartheid legislation to legally prohibit mixed sport. This strategy developed over a period of some years. In 1960, for example, Sewsunker Papwa Sewgolam, an Indian South African golfer, entered for the white-organised Natal Open Golf Championships and, again, in 1963 entered for the Natal and South African Open Golf Championships.

In 1963, the Lincoln City Football Club (of Pietermaritzburg, Natal), which consisted of five Coloureds, four Indians and two whites, played against an Indian team at Curries Fountain, Durban. The Coloured and white members of the team were charged with 'illegally occupying' property zoned for Indians. The Natal Supreme Court dismissed the case. The prosecution's appeal was also lost. Prior to this, black cricketers, footballers and tennis players had played with and against whites.

As late as 1973, the multiracial Aurora Cricket Club of Natal applied, and was accepted, to play in the all-white Pietermaritzburg and District Cricket Union League. The Security Branch of the South African police attended nearly all its matches but did not take any action. The Aurora Cricket Club continued to play in the all-white league, but no charges were ever brought against its players.

Government policy statements
By and large sport in South Africa is determined and administered by general government policy and practice rather than by specific legislation.

The first government guideline was announced in 1956 by the then South African Minister of the Interior who stated that whites and blacks should organise their sporting activities separately, with no inter-racial competition allowed.

Since then the ruling National Party government has made frequent policy announcements. Although a particular statement may seem to differ from its immediate predecessor and is often publicised internationally by the South

African government's propaganda machine as a 'break-through in sport', the essential elements of the National Party's policy of race discrimination are always strongly emphasized.

The main purpose of such policy announcements is to avoid international isolation on the sports field. Quite frequently these announcements are made just before or after major international congresses or sports events where South Africa's race policies have been the focus of attention.

In 1967, for example, when South Africa's participation in the forthcoming Mexico Olympic Games of 1968 was under threat, the Prime Minister, B. J. Vorster, announced that blacks could be part of the South African team but that separate trials for whites and blacks would be held to select its members. He also stated, however, that there could be 'no compromise negotiations or abandonment of principles.'

In 1971, when the international campaign for South Africa's sports isolation was beginning to gain momentum, the South African Prime Minister announced that blacks would be allowed to participate in certain sports events in South Africa which would duly be termed 'multi-national' or open international events.

Motives and intentions

The aims and intentions of the South African government's sports policy are perhaps best illustrated by the words of the ruling minority itself—through excerpts from debates in South Africa's all-white parliament. What is said here, as distinct from statements and announcements composed for the edification of the international sporting community, the press and media, reveals the National Party's continuing commitment to strict racial segregation and discrimination.

'Precisely because it is our declared policy—the world knows it—that we will not in this country allow competition between whites and non-whites on the playing fields.'
(P M K Le Roux – Minister of the Interior - Debates, 8 February 1967).

'The Springbok colours are for white sportsmen only.'
(F W Waring – Minister of Sport and Recreation - Debates, 12 May 1971).

'Separate participation in sport is a natural and obvious outcome of the Government's policy of separate development. It is therefore wrong to speak of a new sport policy or a different formula or certain concessions. However, it is in fact correct to speak of a developing policy which was applied and is being applied to new situations.'
(Dr P J Koornhof – Minister of Sport and Recreation - Debates, 25 May 1973).

'Announcements in respect of certain points of departure relating to sport should therefore be seen as adjustments, development and progress

without sacrifice of principles . . . In a young country like South Africa there has been a certain degree of elasticity, for one has to deal with and control the situation here in a realistic way under all circumstances, as the National Party Government is still doing, particularly against the background that we will not allow and do not want to allow ourselves to be isolated from the international world in the field of sport, or in any sphere whatsoever, as our enemies are trying to do. We do not want to be isolated, and the National Party will make its contribution towards ensuring that this does not happen.'
(Dr P J Koornhof – Minister of Sport and Recreation - Debates, 25 May 1973).

'For an examination of the developing sports policy it is therefore of importance that the policy should be seen in its entirety. But it happens that people quite frequently single out portions of this policy, as it suits them, and read into those certain concessions which do not exist at all. The interpretation of the sport policy should constantly be consistent with the country's fundamental policy of separate development. If this is not done, it is not only erroneous and meaningless, but also causes confusion.'
(Dr P J Koornhof – Minister of Sport and Recreation - Debates, 25 May 1973).

'The National Party reaffirms its well known standpoints on sport as formulated in 1976 as general and fundamental guidelines to be pursued wherever practicable. Exceptional circumstances do not always permit of consistent implementation of the mentioned guidelines and it is recognized that special arrangements are justified in such circumstances. But unnecessary deviations must be guarded against, and exceptions must be dealt with in such a way that they do, in fact, prove the rule.'
(F W de Klerk – Minister of Sport and Recreation - Debates, 21 May 1979).

Laws affecting mixed sport
The South African authorities can make use of the provisions in a wide range of apartheid laws to obstruct mixed sport. The following laws, however, have some direct relation to sport and have been pin-pointed by several legal experts as the major hurdles in the way of mixed sport:

Population Registration Act (No 30 of 1950)
The Act provides for a rigid system of race classification. It defines 'White', 'Coloured', 'Indian' and 'Native' people within the South African population.
'Native' people, also known as 'Bantu' in South African apartheid terminology, are referred to in this book as 'Africans' where it is necessary to distinguish them from other groups. The term 'black' is otherwise used throughout the book to refer collectively to all South Africans other than

those defined as 'White'. In recent years, the South African government has added to the confusion surrounding apartheid terms by using 'Black' to refer specifically to African ('Bantu' or 'Native') people.

'Coloured' people include those deemed by the South African government to be of mixed racial origin, and those of Malaysian and Indonesian descent.

Both the 'Coloured' and the 'Natives' defined in the Act are sub-divided according to ethnic groups.

Group Areas Act (No 36 of 1966 and Proclamations R26 of 1965 and R228 of 1973)

This Act imposed control throughout South Africa over inter-racial property transactions and inter-racial changes of land occupation. It divides South Africa into areas of occupancy and residency according to race. It is also used to prohibit individuals of another race group from remaining in the demarcated race zone (Group Areas) for longer than specified or from attending an entertainment or partaking of any refreshments as a customer.[1]

Reservation of Separate Amenities Act (No 49 of 1953)

This provides that any person who is in charge of or who has control of any public premises or public vehicles may whenever he deems it expedient, reserve such premises or vehicle or any portion thereof for the exclusive use of persons belonging to a particular race or class. Such action cannot be ruled invalid on grounds that provision is not made for all races.[2]

Representatives of foreign Governments and members of their families, together with nations of foreign countries travelling in South Africa on official business are exempted from the provisions of this Act.[3]

This exemption converts foreign blacks into 'honorary whites' during their stay in South Africa. Several black American sportsmen, including tennis star Arthur Ashe, have been welcomed in South Africa under this dispensation.

Bantu Laws Amendment Act (No 76 of 1963)

This Act prohibits the entry of non-Africans into an African location, village or hostel without the permission of the officer in charge. An officer may eject any person whose presence therein is considered to be undesirable.

Native Laws Amendment Act (No 36 of 1957)

This Act provides for the withholding of permission for Africans attending functions, gatherings, etc. outside the so-called native residential areas if that is likely, in the opinion of the Minister of Native Affairs (now the Minister of Plural Relations), to cause a nuisance or is otherwise deemed undesirable.

Native (Urban Areas) Consolidation Act (No 25 of 1945)

This Act, now known as the Blacks (Urban Areas) Consolidation Act, empowers any local authority to make regulations, requiring the approval of the Administrator and the Minister, providing for the prohibition or regulation of the entry or sojourn in a location, native village, or hostel of any person not resident therein.

Liquor Amendment Act (No 58 of 1975 and No 87 of 1977)

In keeping with the South African government's 're-adjusted' policy on sport, the Liquor Act, which originally barred all mixed drinking, was slightly amended during the 1970s. The new legislation, by way of permits, provides for special dispensations (which could be withdrawn at any time) for certain authorised sports functions. It also laid the basis for 'international hotels', wherein the visitor is shielded from the normal apartheid conventions of racial segregation *(see also Ch. 5)*.

The absence of legislation explicitly preventing mixed sport has had advantages for the South African government. It is possible for white sports administrators to introduce a few carefully executed deviations which allow for a few blacks to join white clubs and vice-versa. The aim is to provide the outside world with photographic evidence that mixing of races takes place on South African sportsfields. Special sporting events can be staged for international consumption by issuing permits or licences which normally expire about an hour after the termination of the sports meeting. If there was direct legislation prohibiting mixed sport, South Africa would less easily be able to sugar-coat its policy of racial discrimination. It would less easily be able to insert token black members into its overseas delegations for parading at international congresses. The lack of direct legislation can in short be seen as an ingredient in the South African government's strategy to ward off total isolation.

The sports events arranged or sponsored by the regime for international audiences can usually rely on securing fulsome press and media coverage. Even South Africa's former Minister of Sport and Recreation, Dr P J Koornhof, speaking in 1977, agreed that newspapers 'blew-up' these cases of exceptions, giving a wrong impression of what was going on in the country. He said that 99.9956 per cent of sport was played in terms of the Government's segregated sports policy, and that up to June 1977 there had been only 56 cases of people joining clubs of other racial groups. He also stated that every such case was first brought to him before being executed.[4]

Earlier, he had stated that the deviation represented a minute 0.0045 of the active sport-playing population, but warned that the Government might be forced to take action if the policy was contravened too often.[5]

During 1981-82, the South African government introduced further changes and amendments into the administrative dispensations for sport. The Liquor Amendment Act, the Group Areas Act and the Native (Urban Areas) Consolidation Act, were, or were due to be, amended so as to formalise their provisions relating to sport without actually changing their substance. These 'reforms' are discussed in Chapter 5, MANOEUVERS TO BREAK OUT OF ISOLATION.

Document II: An example of the procedures involved for black sports bodies wishing to arrange events — letter from Pretoria City Secretary concerning the lease of Caledonian Stadium

Stadsraad van Pretoria
City Council of Pretoria
Afdeling van die Stadsekretaris
Department of the City Secretary
12 June 1980

By registered post

The Honorary Secretary
Northern Transvaal Football Association
PO Box 66
PRETORIA
0001

Sir

LEASE IN RESPECT OF CALEDONIAN STADIUM

I am writing with reference to the incident which occurred on Saturday, 24 May 1980 at the above stadium, details of which are peculiarly within your knowledge and previous incidents of a similar nature.

You will appreciate that in the interest of the citizens and ratepayers of Pretoria, my Council cannot allow a recurrence of these incidents and that it has no option but to take whatever steps in its power to prevent such a recurrence.

In the circumstances my Council has resolved that in so far as it may be necessary you be formally notified, as I hereby do, that it requires strict adherence to the provisions to clause 1 of the lease in respect of each and every match played at the said stadium to which the said clause applies.

Any match played at the stadium in breach of clause 1 of the lease will be regarded as breach of contract in which event my Council will apply the provisions of clause 25 and terminate the lease forthwith.

This letter is written against the background of my Council's information that of the future soccer matches which are scheduled to be played on the leased premises may constitute a breach of clause 1 of the lease.

Under the circumstances and considering the urgency and import of the problem referred to in the 1st paragraph hereof, my Council requires your undertaking and guarantee that no match will be played in contravention of the said clause 1.

In order to resolve the matter in sufficient time, my Council requires the said undertaking and guarantee in writing with a copy of the relevant resolution by your governing body, authorizing the undertaking and guarantee, to reach this office not later than 20 June 1980.

It must be pointed out that should the said undertaking and guarantee not be received as stated, all my Council's rights, including the right to apply for an interdict on an urgent basis, are fully reserved.

Yours faithfully

CITY SECRETARY

SUBJECT TO THE FOLLOWING TERMS AND CONDITIONS:

1)   The leased premises shall be used by the Lessees for the purpose of playing football thereon, arranging and exhibiting football games thereon, and enabling the public to witness such games and matches and generally for the purpose of football grounds, provided that no football matches between non-European football teams be held on the grounds without the prior consent in writing of the Lessors being had and obtained provided that no football match in which one or more non-European players participate shall be held on the leased premises without the prior consent in writing of the Lessors, which consent shall not be given unless it has been authorised by the Administrator as defined in Section 2 of the Local Government Ordinance, No 17 of 1939, as amended.

3. Repression

South Africa is at pains to point out that sport in the country is 'normalised'. Meanwhile, the authorities systematically suppress all opposition to the country's 'multi-national' sports policy. Anyone who dares to expose their fraud is persecuted and intimidated.

As a general rule blacks are extremely cautious about publishing their opposition to apartheid because opposition can mean dismissal from employment, visits by the police at all hours of the day and night, or transportation to the 'homelands'. Many blacks, naturally, are not prepared to risk their 'bread and butter' positions.

As far as sport is concerned, such measures ensure that the stated government policy of 'multi-national' sport is strictly adhered to, and that any propagation of genuine non-racial sport is suppressed.

Legal harassment

The regime makes use of the apartheid statute book, particularly laws relating to geographical segregation and zoning, to obstruct racially mixed sports events and generally make life difficult for the advocates of non-racial sport. The need to protect 'law and order' is frequently cited, too, as a means of clamping down on mixed events.

The case of professional football is a good example. Here, even the officially-approved 'multi-national' events ran into trouble when the authorities decided that their own policies of 'reform' were being implemented too enthusiastically.

After the government-authorised National Professional Soccer League (NPSL), which contained both black and white teams, got under way in the late 1970s it was realised that player and crowd control were breaking down. There was violence both on and off the field, and administration was becoming very lax. Matches never began on time or were even cancelled altogether, and whites became concerned.

Most of the clubs in the NPSL at its inception were black and not much interest had ever been shown by South African whites in professional football. This motivated the Government to force professional football into the black townships, thereby discouraging white participation even further.

During the early stages of multi-national professional football white entry into the black townships was controlled by a strict quota system which stipulated that a 'maximum of 30 white spectators comprising officials and other interested parties are allowed to accompany a team'.[1]

The present regulations came into force in early 1980 when it was announced in the South African Parliament that

'In order to facilitate the attendance by all races at sporting events within urban black residential areas the entrance tickets to such sporting events are regarded as adequate to enable non-blacks to enter such areas provided, however, that the relevant administration board and the South African Police are informed in advance about the event and that the admission tickets are purchased beforehand.'[2]

It was intended during 1982 to insert this regulation in the amendment of the Blacks (Urban Areas) Consolidation Act *(see Ch. 5)*.

The ultimate decision to permit racial mixing by both players and fans always rests with some department of the apartheid Government. In all instances the number of non-blacks entering black areas is effectively controlled by the respective administration board.

In 1979, for example, the Johannesburg City Council banned professional football at the Rand Stadium, the foremost football stadium in South Africa, located in a white residential area, under the guise that it was getting too small for the large crowds attending the matches.

A similar excuse was expounded by a senior white South African rugby official when the Pretoria City Council banned a professional football club from using the City's Caledonian Stadium. 'The stadium is simply too small for spectator control', he maintained, 'and it is not the responsibility of the City Council to provide new facilities at its own expense for professional sport.'[3].

The chairman of the Pretoria football club nevertheless reiterated that: 'The true facts are that black players, amateur or professional, are not permitted by the Pretoria City Council to play on any of their fields with the exception of the Caledonian Stadium where, according to their infamous Clause One, which is still in existence, black amateurs may play, or practise, but only under the condition that the club concerned submits a written application to the Pretoria City Council in a match-to-match basis'[4] *(See Document II)*.

Even where the Government authorises certain events to become mixed the holding of such events is further screened by municipal authorities, which own most facilities, so as to ensure compliance with local racial policies.

Two City Councils, for example, Krugersdorp and Newcastle, refused point blank to give permission to hold mixed boxing matches at any of their facilities. This took place as recently as July 1981.[5]

Sports clubs and associations are often willing partners in these manoeuvres. The chairman of South Africa's Association of Sports Clubs, for example, warned its affiliated clubs not to accept blacks as members. White club managers pointed out that they themselves could be prosecuted by autonomous local authorities if they agreed to admit blacks as members.[6]

In other cases, clubs and local authorities find themselves at loggerheads.

In January 1981, the Oudtshoorn Town Council rejected an application from its cricket club for a permit which would have allowed a Coloured to play cricket on the municipal sports ground.[7]

A black trampolinist, participating within the parameters of the Government's multi-national policy, was in 1981 barred from training at a sports hall after the Johannesburg Council received a complaint that a black person was using equipment in a white sports centre. This was despite the fact that the trampolinist was Transvaal champion and was due to promote South Africa's cause by competing in the world trampolining championships in the USA in May 1982. As a special 'privilege', he was allowed to practise at the whites-only Oribi Recreation Centre at specific times, on condition that he was accompanied by his white coach and used the facilities only when whites were not present.[8]

Police persecution

Organisations and persons who openly oppose the Government's sports policy are subjected to more ruthless forms of repression, ranging from restrictions on freedom of movement to fines, arrest and detention.

In July 1981, for example, the secretary of the anti-apartheid South African Council on Sport (SACOS) was invited to New York by the United Nations Special Committee Against Apartheid to update records. A few days before his departure two members of the Security Branch of the South African Police walked into his office and took away his passport. A month later another member of the Special Branch turned up to enquire about SACOS's activities regarding its opposition to the Springbok rugby tour of New Zealand.

An Oudtshoorn teacher and sports administrator was stopped by police on many occasions when returning from meetings of the South African Council on Sport and in October 1981 the security police 'raided' his house and confiscated several documents and books.[9]

Opponents of the system are told in no uncertain terms of the lines of demarcation when it comes to participating in mixed sport.

In 1977 three members of the white Eastern Province Rugby Union decided to play and coach in the black Kwazakele Rugby Union (KWARU). They were from that date subjected to frequent police harassment and charged several times for being in a black area without a permit. The president of the white, internationally-recognised South African Rugby Board confessed that these players had been banned by his board on the instruction of the Government's Department of Sport.

In August 1981 Gavin van Eyck, captain of the anti-apartheid KWARU, was charged with four others for entering a black township without a permit. They were going to a rugby match in the township and were stopped at a police roadblock.[10]

When questioned in Parliament the Minister of Police said that van Eyck had been charged with contravening section 9(a)(b) of the Blacks (Urban

Areas) Consolidation Act (No 25 of 1945) and that an admission of guilt had been fixed. Should van Eyck fail to pay, he would have to appear in court on 2 September 1981.[11]

The hard fact is that sport in the South African black community is not a 'bread and butter' issue. Many capable and talented black sportsmen and women thus understandably decide that the goal of non-racial sport, however desirable in principle, is not sufficiently fundamental to make it worth risking their livelihoods. They consequently opt to be assimilated into the system or to drop out of the sports scene altogether, rather than to endure police harassment.

In November 1978, Mr Sorgat, an anti-apartheid sports administrator, reluctantly resigned from cricket administration because of constant police intimidation.

Sylvia Coles, a British paraplegic sportswoman, who was resident in South Africa during 1978, later described a subtle case of intimidation within one of South Africa's white sports disciplines, in a personal memorandum to SAN-ROC:

March 1978 - National Paraplegic Games - Cape Town

'These games were 'observed' by some members from overseas countries. I personally met Sir Ludwig Guttman, Miss Scruton, Mrs Dorothy Allott and a gentleman from Sweden.*

My meeting with them took place in the middle of the last night party and prize-giving ceremony, not an ideal place for a serious discussion. However, Miss Scruton did ask me my opinion of the extent of multi-racialism in disabled sport in South Africa, to which I replied that it was probably true at national executive meetings but I had found almost no evidence of it at club level. Because of the circumstances this was the full extent of the conversation.

I returned to Johannesburg the following morning. At about 10.00 pm that same evening I received a phone call from Menzo Barrish (South African National Chairman) to find out what I had said to Miss Scruton, because she had called a special meeting of observers and the National Executive that afternoon to find out whether clubs were, in fact, multi-racial, as the observers had been led to believe. Menzo Barrish was furious that I should have made the remark to Miss Scruton and after much argument I agreed to write to her indicating that I was referring to my observations of the Mandeville Sports and Social Club only. This I did, but also sent a copy to Menzo Barrish together with a suggestion that the national executive investigate the Mandeville Sports and Social Club.

I agreed to write this letter to Miss Scruton because I was honestly

---

* Members of a mission to South Africa from the International Sports Organisation for the Disabled (ISOD).

afraid. South Africa is a police state, and informers are everywhere willing to report anti-South African 'behaviour' to the security police. I have personally met three people who have been interrogated by these police and all have stated that it was a terrifying and frightening experience. They were made aware that not only they, but also their families, might suffer from police surveillance. I was not prepared to put my parents at risk (they were in South Africa at that time) nor did I want to be interrogated myself. In the light of the number of people who have 'accidentally' died during such interrogations, I am not ashamed to admit my fear.'[12]

Document III: Police surveillance of anti-apartheid sports bodies — the experience of a swimming official

Western Cape Amateur Swimming Association

Affilated to SOUTH AFRICAN AMATEUR SWIMMING FEDERATION

CORRESPONDENCE TO THE SECRETARY — 425 VOORTREKKER — MAITLAND — PHONE 51-8529

8th May 1980

The President,
South African Amateur Swimming Federation,
P.O. Box 48178,
QUALBERT,
4078.

Dear Mr. Naidoo,

I wish to bring to your attention the following incidents over the part month:

Thursday, 3 April 1980 - two security branch men called at the Wynberg Swimming Pool to speak to the Superintendent. In the absence of the Superintendent, they spoke to the Assistant Superintendent and wanted to know if they knew of my activities.

Tuesday, 8 April 1980 - the same two men called again, one by the name of Steenkamp. The Superintendent was absent again and on this occasion they spoke to the cashier. They spent half an hour talking and inspecting the pool and its ablution block.

Thursday, 10 April 1980 - the two men called again and found the Superintendent, Mr Rockman. They posed a number of questions to Mr. Rockman about our swimming activities and about myself. On the three occasions a bulky brief case was held by the one man.

Tuesday, 15 April 1980 - I phoned Mr Eric Barlow and asked him to accompany me to Wynberg Pool to discuss the visits with the Pool officials. The following are a few of the questions asked by the policemen.

* What is the procedure for hiring the pool?
* Where are bookings made?

- ★ Are there many spectators who watch swimming?
- ★ Are there enough chairs?
- ★ Do we complain about the lack of facilities?
- ★ Does Mr Ellick ever address the spectators?
- ★ What time do the galas end and does Mr Ellick address groups after the gala?
- ★ Are there any meeting rooms at the pool?
- ★ Who is Mr Ellick's secretary?
- ★ Where does he do his typing and circulars?
- ★ What do you know about SACOS?
- ★ Does Mr Ellick attend SACOS meetings?
- ★ Does he talk about SACOS policies?

The pool employees told the police that they are not connected with Western Cape and don't know much of their activities.

The police told the pool employees they would come again for information. These visits have left both Eric and myself stone cold.

Tuesday, 6 April* 1980 - A certain Mr Steyn of the Department of Sport and Recreation phoned me and said he got my number from Mrs Heeger. Mr Steyn is trying to contact club coaches to arrange a meeting with Mr Bob Campbell who is the National Liaison Officer of the South African Amateur Swimming Union. They want to talk to all 'Coloured', 'Indian' and 'African' clubs about improving swimming in South Africa. I told Mr Steyn he was talking to the wrong organisation as we are non-racial and do not label people according to their race and that he should talk to his racial WPASA where he'll find his stooges. I told him not to talk to any of our clubs or its members. I further told him we have an instruction from our National body not to liaise with SAASU, its units or his Department.

Wednesday, 7 April* 1980 - Whilst preparing for a Western Cape meeting, the telephone rang and Joy (Mr Ellick's daughter) answered. The caller spoke Afrikaans and told Joy it was Mr Barlow and that he wanted to talk to me. When I answered the phone, the caller used abusive language and threatened to smash me. I immediately contacted Eric and told him What had happened. Eric had no knowledge of the phone call.

The above is for your information and if there are any future happenings I'll let you know.

Your sincerely,

R.A. ELLICK
*sic.

Document IV: Impromptu Interrogation—an example from the South African Council on Sport

On 6 August 1981 Major Joseph Benjamin, attached to the South African Special Branch, called unheralded on the Secretary of the South African Council on Sport, M N Pather, at the latter's office. According to a written report subsequently prepared by the SACOS Secretary, Major Benjamin asked the following questions, and received the following replies:

1. How many meetings were held by SACOS since May of this year?
   (Only one)
2. What was the nature of the meeting?
   (Executive)
3. What 'serious' matters were discussed?
   (None)

4. What 'serious' matters were discussed with regard to Rugby?
   (None—all matters are normal matters)
5. What strategies were discussed with regard to the stopping of the present Rugby tour?
   (None)
   (This question was repeated on more than one occasion)
6. What decisions are to be conveyed or have been conveyed to overseas?
   (All matters discussed at meetings are fully publicised and as usual these reports are circulated both locally and internationally, along with other reports concerning sport)
7. Who had come down to the meeting from Kimberley?
   (No one)
8. How many people attended the meeting, when, where?
   (Executive totalled nine, on Sunday 12 July, at this office)
9. Who are the Executive?
   (Various people drawn from the Cabinet and general membership)
10. Were any Resolutions taken at this meeting to stop the tour?
    (No)
11. Do you take the decisions yourself?
    (That depends)
12. Your wife applied for a passport?
    (Yes)
13. Where is she going to?
    (London, Madras, Singapore)
14. Will you use her as your 'Courier'?
    (No need to—as you know all our mail which is scrutinised by the Post Office is sent in the ordinary manner)
15. Don't you use Couriers?
    (Not unless I have to carry it myself)
16. Have you applied for a passport?
    (Yes)
17. Where to?
    (London)

There was then a sort of general discussion on the questions already asked.

M N Pather (signed)
Secretary: South African Council of Sport (SACOS)
13 August 1981

4. Accomplices of the State

'They that can give up essential liberty to obtain a little safety deserve neither liberty nor safety.'

Benjamin Franklin

From the time South Africa was first threatened with expulsion from international sport, the regime has systematically sought out blacks who are prepared to collaborate—or who are unable to avoid doing so—with its policies, and has used them to promote apartheid sport. In this it has enjoyed a certain measure of success.

During the late 1950s white sports administrators began creating disunity among various black groups by requesting municipal authorities to close sports facilities to non-racial bodies on the ground that the latter (which were predominantly or entirely black) were violating the Government's Group Areas Act.

As one sports ground after another was closed to non-racial sports organisations the White Football Association of South Africa created a black football splinter body in Johannesburg and named it the South African Bantu Football Association. B P Morola, President of this splinter body, was taken to the 1962 FIFA (International Football Federation) Congress in Chile. He became the first black spokesman to plead the case of a white sports organisation at an international conference. Although the white Football Association of South Africa would not allow any black or black team to participate in white leagues, Morola told the FIFA Congress:

'Our problem in South Africa will be solved only with time, goodwill and man's natural evolution of thinking and tolerance. It cannot be imposed from outside, and the world in trying to help us should not put too much pressure on us.'[1]

The South African government refused passports to representatives of the anti-apartheid South African Soccer Federation who wanted to put an alternative view to the FIFA Congress.

The 'Bantu' Association has since been renamed the South African National Football Association (SANFA) and its President, George Thabe, has continued to plead the case of South Africa's whites at football congresses and at the Olympic Games.

Those black sports administrators who make statements expressing support for apartheid sport or arguing against an international boycott tend

33

to belong to the ambitious business or merchant class or to be in compromised positions. Most of them are employed by the State or by white-owned businesses which propagate apartheid. It is not surprising that these black officials can be persuaded to support white sports bodies. Quite often these blacks also make their way up, or are conscripted, into state apartheid institutions. George Thabe, for example, was the Chairman of the Vaal Triangle Community Council—an organ of the Government's Ministry of Cooperation and Development (Plural Relations).[2]

The South African government's black spokesmen tend to be career-orientated, articulate and sophisticated. They have developed a subtle, low-key approach to South Africa's race problems. White South Africa's latest strategy in this regard is to form 'umbrella bodies' which, while consistent with apartheid policies, have an elected black president, vice-president or secretary. *De facto* control, however, remains in the hands of whites. It is seemingly hoped that these so-called 'umbrella' racial organisations, developed during the late 1970s, will appear credible because they are being defended by black spokesmen.

'Certain kinds of sport such as athletics, rugby and several others have already established such umbrella bodies. My department and I are continually working in this direction and we give valuable advice and assistance to the sports bodies, because it is in accordance with policy that such umbrella bodies should be established on which the various population groups should be represented.'[3]

A few former advocates of anti-apartheid sport have subsequently emerged as proponents of government policy. In this respect, sport reflects more general changes in South African society. Be it in respect of the bantustans, the Coloureds or the Indians, the regime has taken steps to discover and promote blacks who are willing to serve as instruments of its policy. Whatever the latter's motives, government machinery is strong enough to keep them in check. On 18 May 1977, for example, the Minister of Sport and Recreation explained in the white South African parliament that a 'well-known person who has become known in South Africa as a non-racialist, Mr Varachia, is presently touring abroad to put in a good word for South Africa because we have found and understood one another around the conference table.'[4].

Those prepared to collaborate with the regime, however, ultimately find that they will never be fully accepted into the white system. In 1981, for example, the South African government organised various sports events to commemorate the 20th anniversary, in May of that year, of the founding of the Republic. When it came to the organisation of football fixtures this prestigious position was wrested out of the hand of the umbrella Football Council of South Africa, whose president was black. Instead the organisation was delegated to the white Football Association of South Africa.

Again, in June 1981, the South African Cricket Union sought some form of official government assurance that certain laws affecting mixed sport would shortly be amended. The black president of the Union was ignored and the South African Prime Minister instead wrote officially to its white vice-president explaining the Government's position *(see Document V)*.

South Africa has on several occasions included a single black player in its otherwise all-white national rugby team. Several overseas sportsmen have tried to elicit his feelings on how he felt about being included in the Springbok rugby team but they have all failed. It seems that those black players who co-operate with the apartheid system are constantly watched in case they expose the cover-up.

Tony Ward, an Irish international rugby player, who toured South Africa with the Lions in 1980 but refused to tour with the Irish team in 1981 because he concluded that he was providing apartheid with respectability, had this to say about the only black rugby Springbok:

'But he had his feelings too, and when we were talking together he was always very careful and very conscious as to who was around him and might be listening. One felt he longed to speak his mind but he couldn't.'[5]

In contrast to the treatment accorded to those prepared to co-operate with the regime, South African sportsmen and sports administrators who have genuinely opposed the system have always been refused permission to leave the country to put their case to the world. Those who have stood up for the principle of non-racial sport, furthermore, have not only had to face police persecution but also have jeopardised their jobs and careers.

Document V: Letter from the South African Prime Minister to the Vice-president of the South African Cricket Union

REPUBLIC OF SOUTH AFRICA

Mr Boon Wallace
Vice President of the
South African Cricket Union
44 Stanford Road
RONDEBOSCH 7700

Prime Minister's Office
Private Bag X193
CAPE TOWN
8000
1981-06-12

Dear Mr Wallace

I was pleased to learn from the Minister of National Education about the renewed approach which you and your colleagues of the South African Cricket Union propose to make during July to the International Cricket Council in order to obtain re-admission for South Africa to international cricket.

I should like to send you my very best wishes for success. I trust that your efforts will be promoted by the recently announced decision of the Government to introduce amending legislation in order expressly to exclude sporting events from the application of three laws considered to infringe the autonomy of sporting bodies to organise multi-racial sport. For reference I enclose a copy of the press release in which the Minister of National Education announced this decision.

I should like to give you the assurance that cricket teams invited by your Union from any country abroad will be most wecome in South Africa.

Yours sincerely

PRIME MINISTER

35

5. Manoeuvres to Break Out of Isolation

Sport has always played a significant role in South Africa's search for international respectability. In a parliamentary debate in May 1977, the South African Minister of Sport made it clear that sport, far from being a side-issue, played a crucial role in foreign relations:

'. . . we want to compete internationally and we are going to compete internationally . . . Let us admit here this afternoon that play and sport are strong enough to cause political and economic relations to flourish or collapse . . . We are not holding on to it just because we fear expulsion, but also and specially because of the value of sport on the international level.'[1]

The campaign to exclude South Africa from international sport is equally significant because it affects one of the major outlets for the aggrandisement of apartheid and white supremacy. The boycott campaign has forced South Africa to make constant re-adjustments to its racial policies in the hope of being re-admitted into international sport. These adjustments have been initiated as part of the South African government's general programme of 'multi-racialism' or 'multi-nationalism'—or in other words, apartheid. The special value of sport in lending credibility to the overall 'grand design' of the apartheid state was aptly summed up in the same debate by the Minister of Sport:

'By means of sport, a new dimension is being given to our policy of multinationalism and to the South African set-up which, since 1652, has been in embryo what it has become today. We should not lose sight of the fact that we are dealing here with a historic situation. Within the framework of this historic situation, as well as of other circumstances in South Africa, sport is being used to create a spirit and an attitude which have a positive value, a spirit and an attitude which are giving new dimensions to our multi-national set-up.'[2]

Some months previously, on 23 September 1976, the South African government had announced an eight-point plan for its future sporting policy, clearly directed at the international sporting community.

The eight-point plan
The eight-point plan defined the parameters within which mixed sport would henceforth be permissible. It provided for mixed race events or leagues to be arranged by 'umbrella' sports bodies at national or provincial level, but only

under certain specified circumstances. These were narrowly defined *(see Document VI).*

Immediately after the announcement South Africa's white newspapers hailed the new sports policy as a 'break-through' and claimed that mixed clubs were now permissible. When blacks sought clarification the Department of Sport and Recreation replied as follows:

'In reply I wish to refer you to the press statement which was released on 23 September 1976 on behalf of the Honourable the Prime Minister. The paragraph dealing with your first question, reads as follows: "That the sportsmen and sportswomen of the whites, Coloureds, Indians and Black peoples belong to their own clubs and control, arrange and manage their own sports matters".'

The press statement to which the statement referred further stipulated that the new policy would apply 'with due regard to the provisions of any laws and regulations which may be appropriate. The introduction of the new sports policy has not brought about any changes as far as permits are concerned. Permits will therefore have to be obtained under the circumstances mentioned in your second question'.[3]

Later a further clarification was issued:

'Your players are not allowed to join white clubs. It is for this reason that the sports policy has been changed, namely to give all race groups the opportunity to play against each other on club level and thus sharing the same facilities. Members of each and every population group have to join their own clubs. Outstanding players will have the benefit of playing in provincial and national teams.'[4]

The Minister of Sport and Recreation reaffirmed this policy in the South African parliament on 21 May 1979.

The permit system

Since 1973, the South African government has operated a permit system to allow for selected mixed race sports events. In October 1979, certain reforms were introduced, on the basis of which the regime has claimed that the permit system has been superseded. In fact, that is not strictly true. Only the procedure was altered, while the underlying principle remained the same.

Basically, a series of permits continue to be necessary to get round the myriad of apartheid laws. An application for a mixed race sports event is made to the white Department of Sport and Recreation which monitors all such mixed sports activity. The application is thoroughly scrutinized so as to ensure that all aspects of the government's sports policy are strictly adhered to.

The current practice of the Department of Sport and Recreation is to give a blanket permit for a whole season to selected cricket, football and other organisations. The department retains complete control over such organisations despite any impression they may give of being run by blacks.

Up to October 1979, these organisations still had to make further applications in respect of each fixture, if they wished to admit persons of more than one race group as spectators.

If a black sports body wishes to defy government policy and go ahead without a permit to hold an unauthorised mixed race event its officials are warned about the consequences—usually loss of the sports field, loss of employment, etc. If this does not work the police disrupt the event and transport the offenders to a police station for questioning. Usually no charge is brought against the sports officials but this form of constant intimidation compels the 'offenders' to follow government policy.

Readjustments in 1979

Towards the end of the 1970s, the permit system, with all its cumbersome restrictions, began to attract increasingly adverse and critical publicity. The South African government responded by further readjusting its policy through a circular issued on 27 October 1979. The circular stated that in future 'all sports activities will be disassociated from the Group Areas Act, that is to say no permit, as required by the Act, is in any manner applicable to sport.' It continued by explaining that 'the autonomy of sports bodies and owners of sports facilities is fully acknowledged and as a result thereof, the onus of approval or refusal of occupation will mainly rest with the owner (private and/or local authority) of the venue and the respective sports body'. *(The full text of the circular is given in Document VII).*

The onus for taking decisions about racial segregation was, in effect, shifted from the state to local authorities, private bodies and individuals—a device which, in other contexts besides that of sport, has enabled the *status quo* to be retained behind a facade of apparent reform.

On the basis of the circular's provisions, the government claimed that sport in South Africa was now completely normalised and that permits were no longer necessary to play mixed sport. The government's position that 'the autonomy of sports bodies in respect of sports is recognised' is constantly quoted by South Africa's supporters. However, the government's pre-condition, as it was stated earlier in 1979 in parliament for example, 'that good order does not suffer and that the general laws of the country are recognised', tends to be omitted.[5] The 'general laws of the country' are the apartheid laws which are detested the world over and which make the playing of mixed sport at all levels impossible.

South Africa's new sports policy as announced on 27 October 1979 was just old wine poured into a new bottle. The Sports Minister himself reiterated in the circular that the new situation

> 'involves no policy change but only a change in procedure aimed at streamlining the present system.'[6]

The change in procedure seems to have been prompted by the need to replace the apartheid word 'permit' by more subtle and acceptable words for international consumption. The words 'consultation' and 'co-operation' are now official words for permits. The regime had previously made it clear that 'unnecessary deviations must be guarded against and exceptions must be dealt with in such a way that they do, in fact, prove the rule.'[7]

The most important aspect of the adjusted sports policy is that this dispensation was and remains only valid for organised sport. Recreation and leisure activities, together with facilities for training, remain strictly segregated.

The owners of sports facilities are not authorised to admit blacks for recreational purposes other than for special events. Therefore, for example, a swimming pool may be out of bounds to blacks for training although black swimmers may be allowed to compete there at a 'multi-national' competition.

The government strategy merely altered the instruments of discrimination, without abolishing discrimination itself. Indeed, a number of local authorities subsequently refused permission for the holding of mixed sports events, despite the fact that these were authorised by the government. When questioned the Minister of Sport and Recreation explained that such actions were within the ambit of the 1979 dispensation. The behaviour of the local authorities concerned was again defended by the the government in the parliamentary debate of 6 March 1982.

The control of sports fields

Nearly all sports facilities in black residential areas are controlled by government departments. The departments have endeavoured over the years to wrest control of such facilities from anti-apartheid bodies and hand responsibility over to persons or groups who are prepared to co-operate with government policy.

Thus, sports facilities in African areas have for a long time been strictly controlled by administration boards. For example, sports grounds in Soweto, the vast black satellite township of Johannesburg, are managed by a government agency, the West Rand Administration Board (WRAB). The WRAB, by careful monitoring, has ensured that sports organisations which overtly oppose government policy are deprived of the use of these facilities.

The government has in similar fashion managed to retain overall control of football, the major sport of interest to the African population. White South Africans are able to boast as a result that the majority of blacks follow the government line when it comes to soccer.

The pervasive government control of sport in African areas means that in practice, most anti-government sports activities have been centred around Coloured or Asian group areas. Here too, agencies have been set up by the state to administer the sports fields. Municipal authorities now tend to hand over exclusive authority to sports bodies which are prepared to co-operate with the government.

For instance, the white Johannesburg City Council handed over to the pro-government Transvaal Cricket Council the exclusive control and use of the Asian cricket grounds of Lenasia. This deprived the anti-government Transvaal Cricket Board of the use of all cricket pitches in the area.[8]

In Soweto the Black Tennis Foundation, a pro-government body, was allowed to take control of all the tennis courts in the township. This forced the anti-apartheid sports groups who were active in the area to concede to the wishes of the government. A further move by the Black Tennis Foundation, which liaises closely with the West Rand Administration Board and the government education departments, put school children into a position where they were obliged to use government or pro-government facilities for coaching clinics. Transport, food and equipment are laid on free in these clinics.[9]

White sports administrators hope by such tactics to maintain control over black tennis players.

In the Cape Province the Cape Town City Council disbanded the Belville Sports Board which had done a reasonable job for 30 years, and instead obliged Coloureds to apply to use the sports grounds through the Proteaville Management Committee, an organ of the South African government.[10] A similar move in Port Elizabeth deprived Coloured cricketers of access to the cricket pitches which they had previously used.[11]

Black visitors
South Africa has realized the value of inviting black sportsmen and women from overseas to visit the country to give credibility to apartheid. It has taken steps to modify certain laws relating to liquor consumption and other matters, to accommodate these blacks who are then expected to return full of praise for the South African system.

The Liquor Amendment Act (No. 58 of 1975, published during 1974), was designed mainly to simplify the procedure for black visitors from other countries. This states that any African, Asian or Coloured person who is a visitor to South Africa may use hotel bars and restaurants without any restrictions. Africans who enter South Africa under a migratory labour scheme are not permitted to use these facilities, however, as they are not considered 'visitors'.[12]

When 'international' and 'multi-national' events are held in South Africa, blacks who are included in the white teams are accommodated in white hotels to give the appearance of equality. To overcome the usual restrictions of apartheid segregation the government has created provisions for the establishment of 'international hotels' inside South Africa. Proprietors of large hotels can apply for a permit to accommodate blacks and supply them with food and liquor. Such permits are now granted very selectively to white hotels on condition that blacks are not allowed to dance or use swimming pools. It is stipulated that not more than five to 15 per cent of the hotel beds may at any time be occupied by black persons.[13]

According to information supplied to the British Sports Council 'some 15 per cent non-whites are allowed to use the hotel at any time—this percentage is decided upon once a year—the licensee decides—some hotels have a 25 per cent ceiling'.[14]

In 1978 a similar provision was granted to some white clubs so that they could admit an occasional black member; and to some white restaurants. As regards sports clubs the 'non-white' must be a 'competitor', 'official' or 'guest' and 'no dancing shall take place in that part of the premises in which such person is present'.[15]

Permits must be renewed annually, at which time each case is thoroughly reviewed by the National Liquor Board. Any club or hotel which on review is found not to be strictly adhering to government regulations loses the privilege.

Permission for clubs of different colour to play against each other is granted by means of a blanket or special permit. Exceptions to the general rule, whereby a few black players are permitted into a white club, are exactly that—exceptions. The new policy seems deliberately designed to confuse people. The 'multi-national' or 'separate development' policy in sport in fact entrenches racialism and is a logical extension of apartheid. The term 'international status' has been very carefully and deliberately chosen to perpetuate the myth of separate 'nations' among the black people. It also suggests, very subtly, an arrangement which is internationally acceptable—which it is *not*.

A little known aspect of the 'new sports policy' is that effective administration and political control of the various sports disciplines have remained in white hands. A black person can in practice only occupy a top administrative post if he or she is prepared to conform to government requirements and overall apartheid policy.

Further amendments
South Africa's latest manoeuvre in its efforts to mask the reality of apartheid sport consisted, in 1981-82, of introducing further amendments to three of the discriminatory laws which affect the daily lives of South Africa's blacks:

* *Liquor Act*
* *Group Areas Act*
* *Blacks (Urban Areas) Consolidation Act*

These amendments to the laws essentially do no more than formalise previous administrative dispensations allowing for the mixing of races at *bona fide* sports events. The *bona fide* events are government-authorised sport events. Reports, photographs and movie films of these events are extensively used as part of the regime's international propaganda exercises to gain respectability for apartheid.

41

The racial mixing provided for under these amendments extends only to the event itself, and no further. For instance, a black might be given permission to take part in a swimming competition in a white pool, but cannot use the pool for training or for recreational swimming.

A black trampolinist, chosen to represent South Africa at an international contest due to be held in the USA in May 1982 was prevented from using the only available recreation centre for training. Adverse publicity then forced the authorities to allow the trampolinist to use the centre once a week for training. The general manager of Johannesburg's Parks and Recreational Department explained that 'the centre's facilities are reserved for whites only, but we would be able to make the necessary arrangement to have him practise on his own'.[16]

The amendment of the three laws was recommended in 1980 by the Human Sciences Research Council of South Africa, in a study commissioned by the South African government. The Human Sciences Research Council accepted the basic tenets of racial segregation:

'Sports autonomy includes the right to differentiate on the basis of factors such as race, culture, religion, language etc'.

'Differentiation as opposed to discrimination means distinction on the basis of a factor that is socially and culturally relevant in the particular circumstances.[17]

In 1980 white South Africa lied to the world by administratively changing the word 'permit' to 'consultation', thereby giving the erroneous impression that 'permits' were no longer required to arrange mixed sports meetings. Now, by administratively substituting the word 'differentiation' for 'discrimination', the regime is hoping to mislead the world into believing that racial discrimination has been eradicated from South African sport.

Following the Human Sciences Research Council's recommendations, South Africa's white sports administrators soon began to defend racial discrimination by stating that they could not interfere with club autonomy.

When two Coloured athletes were barred from athletic clubs on grounds of race, for example, the secretary of the South African Amateur Athletic Union said:

'It's up to the clubs to decide for themselves who to accept and who to reject. Because they are autonomous we can't force them to take on anybody.

'It's the same with clubs in other sports. I believe there is a golf club in Johannesburg who will not allow Jews to join.

'If the two runners can't find a club to join, they can register with the Northern Transvaal association as individuals. I believe this has happened before in the North Western Cape.'[18]

The chairman of one of the clubs confirmed that his club was closed to all but the whites.[19]

The latest amendments are designed to deceive the naive into believing that mixed sport is the order of the day in South Africa. Further, they provide ammunition for supporters of South Africa to argue the case for the re-admission of apartheid sport into the international arena. Undoubtedly, the main motivation in amending these laws was to facilitate the re-entry of white South Africa into international sport.

For example, in clarifying the reason for amending the Liquor Act the Minister responsible stated:

> 'He (*member of opposition*) must keep in mind the position in which South African sportsmen and sporting bodies find themselves in the world today and the almost desperate effort of our sports administrators to retain a foothold in international sport.'[20]

A member of the opposition party in South Africa's all-white parliament, questioning the motives for excluding only *bona fide* sports events from the provisions of the Group Areas Act, stated:

> 'I think the reason is a cynical and sordid little one. I think it is simply because the NP (*ruling National Party*) wants so desperately to get South Africa back into the world of international sport. That is the reason why this is being done, and not because of equal opportunity or because they do not believe in the Group Areas Act, because they do believe in it absolutely. They just miserably want to creep into the arena of world sport.'[21]

The Minister in charge of administering the Group Areas Act referred in his reply to the continuing efforts of sports organisers and administrators to 'do everything in their power to free our young people from the isolation in sport which our enemies want to impose on us every day.' He went on to concede that we have been 'doing these things administratively over the years, to give them a better chance of breaking out of that isolation.'[22]

As they were presented in the press and media, especially for international consumption, the amendments cleverly concealed the continuing racial discrimination in South African sport. The South African government, nevertheless, made it clear in statements intended for its own supporters inside the country that local authorities, which own and control nearly all sports facilities, were free to practice racial discrimination:

> 'The Pretoria city council, for example, imposed restrictions on black people wanting to enter the Caledonian sports stadium in Pretoria. They have the right to do so and they will continue to have the right. The Johannesburg city council entered into a lease with the amateur soccer club in respect of the Rand Stadium. This is a club consisting mainly of white people. However, they refused to enter into a contract with the professional soccer club, which consisted mainly of black people. In this connection, the Johannesburg city council and the Pretoria city council have local option.'[23]

South Africa's white sports administrators work hand-in-glove with government officials to ensure that only minimal racial mixing is effected. The

43

government constantly praises white sports administrators for exercising 'discretion' and for their 'responsible' handling of *bona fide* mixed sports events. While the Government still reserves the right to suspend any conditions of this dispensation, it need not worry too much at the prospect of 'irresponsible' behaviour by its sports administrators. The last all-white election held in South Africa in April 1981 indicated that four fifths of the electorate voted for candidates who wished to retain racial segregation. Considering the general characteristics of participation in South African sports and its administration, this plebiscite can be assumed to also reflect white South Africa's attitude to mixed sport.

In fact, one of South Africa's ruling National Party MPs confidently stated:
'Individuals or clubs that do not wish to compete against other individuals or clubs if people of colour are participating, do not have to. I think that if one were to conduct a poll on this issue amongst the sportsmen and sportswomen of South Africa, one would find them voting overwhelming for this measure.'[24]

When the amendment to the Liquor Act was being discussed in South Africa's all-white parliament in October 1981, an opposition member appropriately summarised the apartheid sports fraud:
'It gives sportsmen—here we are only dealing with sportsmen—a licence to be white for the short time they are engaged in sporting activities, but reduces them to a lower status as soon as they leave the club premises. They cannot go with their team mates to the movies and they cannot ride with their team-mates in the same public transport in most cities in this country. They cannot go with their team-mates in the same trains unless some special arrangements have been made. Unless a hotel in South Africa has been given special permission they cannot stay in such a hotel either. They cannot stay in such hotels, in fact unless somebody telephones the hon. the Minister and gets special permission for them to do so'.[25]

Some months later, during a debate on the amendment to the Group Areas Act the same opposition member, D J Dalling, stated that:
'Some people will argue that the guts of the law still remains. And they will have a valid argument, for the Group Areas Act covers far more than sports fields. Others will argue that normal sport cannot be played in an abnormal society. They will, with justification, point out that it is a personal insult to an individual to be classified a first-class citizen while watching or playing sport, only to be rendered inferior and to be discriminated against as soon as the sports gathering is at an end.'[26]

White South Africans, in their determination to re-enter international sport, as with all other aspects of life under apartheid, do not consider the feelings of black people. The demand by the black majority for equality cannot be satisfied by cosmetic measures which confer equality only during a sports event. Resistance to this cosmetic farce is conveniently defined by white

South Africa as 'being politically motivated'.

The folly of re-adjusting three of the myriad laws of apartheid for the sake of sneaking into international sport was echoed in the South African parliament itself by B B Goodall, an opposition member:

'Can one have normal sport in a society where one has a web of discriminatory legal measures? And those we still have.'[27]

Document VI: The Sports Policy Announcement of 23 September 1976

The Federal Information Council of the National Party accepts that, taking into account the applicable legislation and regulations, the interests of South Africa and all its peoples in respect of sport can best be served in terms of the following policy:

1   White, Coloured, Indian and black sportsmen and women should all belong to their own clubs. Each should control, arrange, and manage its own sporting fixtures.
2   Wherever possible, practical and desirable the committees or councils of the different race groups should consult together or have such contact as would advance the interests of the sport concerned.
3   Inter-group competition in respect of individual types of sport (will) be allowed at all levels, should the controlling bodies so decide.
4   In respect of team sports, the councils or committees of each racial group should arrange their own leagues or programmes within the racial group.
5   Where mutually agreed councils or committees may, in consultation with the Minister, arrange leagues or matches enabling teams from different racial groups to compete.
6   Each racial group should arrange its own sporting relationships with other countries or sporting bodies in accordance with its own wishes, and each should award its own badges and colours.
7   If and when invited or agreed, teams comprising players from all racial groups can represent South Africa, and can be awarded colours which, if so desired, can incorporate the national flag or its colours.
8   Attendance at sporting fixtures can be arranged by the controlling bodies.

Document VII: Circular issued by the South African Department of Sport on 27 October 1979

At a National Sports Administrators' Conference on 27 October, and at a National Press Conference on the same date, Minister Janson again explained the position as far as permits regarding sport were concerned. The complete situation as far as the application of the Group Areas Act, the Urban Areas Act and the Liquor Act is concerned, was explained in a circular which was sent to all National Controlling Bodies of Sport, which reads as follows:

As a result of the recent announcement by the Minister of Sport and Recreation regarding the above, the following is brought to your attention.

The announcement, which was cleared in writing by all the departments concerned, involves no policy change but only a change in procedure aimed at streamlining the present systems. The Acts that have an influence on the practising of sport, will be adapted in such a way that all possible restricting factors will be eliminated.

In order to prevent any misunderstanding and confusion regarding the announcement, the following directives are applicable:

1   **The Group Areas Act**
    According to the new approach, all sports activities will be disassociated from the Group Areas Act, that is to say no permit, as required by this Act, is in any manner applicable to sport.
        The autonomy of sports bodies and owners of sports facilities is fully acknowledged and as a result thereof, the onus of approval or refusal of occupation will mainly rest with the owner (private and/or local authority) of the terrain and the respective sports body. The conditions which were formerly recognised for multinational meetings will henceforth become the decision of the owner of the terrain. These conditions can therefore, according to circumstances, be fully or partially applied or lifted.
        In order to maintain good order, it will be expected of owners and the sports bodies to consult the Department before sports facilities are opened as multinational venues. Every regional office of the Department will therefore, in consultation with the owners, submit a list of sports venues to Head Office, after which these venues will be accepted as an 'interclub' venue for an indefinite period. The only limitation to which this concession will be subject is that in the case of disorder or neglect in any respect, it will be subject to reconsideration.
        All concessions in respect of occupation in regard to sporting activities which take place in a White area, shall therefore in the future, be exclusively dealt with and disposed of by the Department of Sport and Recreation in co-operation with the respective owners. The Department may consult other Departments if it is considered necessary, but the responsibility of making a decision rests with this Department. The unique concession of the Department refers only to the venue and not to the *activity*.
        Mixed school sport is dealt with by each Education Department separately. Only where public facilities are to be used by schools, the concessionary procedures as set out above for competitive sport, will be applied to mixed school sport.

2   **Urban Areas Consolidation Act**
    The following arrangements shall in future apply when allowing Non-Black persons to attend sports meetings within a Black urban residential area:

    Spectators :   An admission ticket will serve as a permit for the specific meeting.
    Participants: A club membership card from the respective club will be regarded as a permit for the specific match.

        The above mentioned arrangement is subject to the condition that the respective Administration Boards and the SA Police are consulted beforehand on the matter and that admission tickets are sold prior to the meeting.

3   **The Liquor Act and mixed club membership**
    No act exists which forbids mixed membership of a sports club. The decision regarding membership and admission to the club's facilities is, and remains, the prerogative of the club itself.
        Furthermore, the Liquor Act does not place any restriction on mixed membership in respect of licensed clubs. Article 72(1) of the Act, however, prohibits the sale or supplying of meals, refreshments, accommodation or liquor to Non-White in on-consumption liquor licensed premises for whites.
        The Minister of Justice can, however, upon request of an on-consumption licensee, authorise the sale or supplying of refreshments, meals, accommodation or liquor on the premises to someone who is a Non-White or allow someone who is a guest on the premises, that is to say the extension of the so-called 'international status'.

46

Furthermore, the Act makes provision that a 'condition' or 'restriction' under which an 'international status' has been authorised, can be amended under special circumstances. If a condition should cause embarrassment or practical problems, the licensee is free to apply to the National Liquor Board for an amendment to the condition or for exemption thereof.

Any application containing a specific need or problem must, as far as possible, be submitted in writing to the Secretary for Justice, Private Bag X81, Pretoria 0001. In urgent cases the application can be made telephonically at 48-3794, Pretoria.

As the Group Areas Act is no longer applicable to sport, an occupation permit shall not serve as a condition for a liquor licence.

(The circular was issued in October 1979 to all government-recognised sports bodies. The text above is as it was later made available by the South African Department of Sport and Recreation to the fact-finding delegation of the British Sports Council in January 1980)

Document VIII: The Recommendations of the Human Sciences Research Council, September 1980

Memorandum concerning the recommendations contained in the report by the Committee for the Jurisprudential Investigation into Legislation that Hampers Sports Relations in the Republic of South Africa (Report No 1 of the National Sports Investigation of the HSRC)

1   **Recommendations with regard to the formulation and implementation of a sports policy**

The findings of the Committee are as follows:

1.1   Recognition in principle of a right to participate in sport.
1.2   It is the right of active participants, sports organizers and spectators to participate.
1.3   Participation in sport is basically an educational, social and cultural activity that includes active participation, organization, watching and the social activities usually associated with sports activities.
1.4   Discriminatory measures such as discriminatory legislation, for example, are regarded as unacceptable in principle in the field of sport.
1.5   The principle of sport autonomy must be maintained and promoted.
1.6   Sports autonomy in principle involves the right of a sports organization to be established at the free will of the founders, free decision-taking regarding membership, free regulation and enforcement of domestic and disciplinary measures, free appointment of officials and the freedom to arrange competitions and make competition-related and/or incidental arrangements.
1.7   Any so-called sports organization openly or secretly working against the interests of sport and thwarting the law, should be regarded as abusing its autonomy and warranting investigation by the authorities.
1.8   Sports autonomy includes the right to differentiate on the basis of factors such as race, culture, religion, language etc.
1.9   Differentiation as opposed to discrimination means distinction on the basis of a factor that is socially and culturally relevant in the particular circumstances.
        (A sports club that aims therefore at admitting only Portuguese or Germans or Whites or Blacks for example, practises differentiation but not discrimination.)
1.10   At this stage in the legal development of the RSA the norm regarding discrimination is not legal or statutory but of a moral nature. Legally speaking, therefore, discrimination is not illegal or unlawful; the value judgement lies at the

moral and ethical level.

1.11 In the formulation and implementation of a sports policy, sport should not be used as a political instrument by the authorities but should in general be supported, promoted and sponsored.

1.12 In the support of sport by the authorities, interference with the autonomy of sport should be guarded against.

1.13 Legislation that does not by nature relate to sports situations (eg the Group Areas Act) should not for example be made applicable to sport by proclamation.

1.14 'Administrative' exemption from legislative measures is legally impermissible and undesirable from a policy-forming point of view.

2 Recommendations with regard to the amendment of legislation

The following is recommended:

2.1 *Group Areas Act (No 36 of 1966)*

2.2 The Act does not apply to sport situations (with the exception of Section 1(4)). However the Committee recommends that in order to prevent uncertainty and even malicious criticism an appropriate proclamation be issued in terms of Section 26(3)(a). An alternative would be to define sports situations as non-occupation of premises in Section 1(1) of the Act.

2.3 In terms of Section 1(4) of the Act, the State President can by proclamation declare the presence of persons on premises reserved for particular purposes mentioned in the proclamation to be illegal occupation. Proclamation R228 of 1973 was issued in terms of this authorization.

The Committee regards the above proclamation as *ultra vires* on account of its vagueness and obscurity. As long as no supreme court judgment has been passed, however, it must be regarded as *prima facie* valid.

The provisions of proclamation R228 affect participation in sport *prima facie* directly and are of a discriminatory nature and purpose.

The Committee therefore recommends that Section 1(4) of the Act as well as Proclamation R228 be repealed (or alternatively not be made applicable to participation in sport).

The Committee stresses the fact that in accordance with administrative practice sports situations are already exempted from the proclamation.

3 Liquor Act (No. 87 of 1977)

3.1 It is the opinion of the Committee that problems regarding the supply of liquor to other racial groups can be obviated by granting exemption under Section 211, the exemption article of the Liquor Act, to *bona fide* sports clubs that are holders of a club or sports ground licence, with the implication that such clubs will not have to apply for exemption in terms of Section 72(3) or 72(4).

The Committee feels that sports clubs should be relied on to take regulatory measures regarding the supply of liquor.

3.2 This recommendation does not entail radical change either. In practice such *ad hoc* exemptions in terms of Section 72(4) are fairly readily granted.

4 Reservation of Separate Amenities Act (No. 49 of 1953)

In the Committee's opinion it would be artificial to exclude only sport from the discriminatory effect of the Act. In the light of this view the Committee feels that this Act in its totality (and not only as applicable to sport), together with other relevant discriminatory legislation, should be subjected to a comprehensive jurisprudential investigation.

48

5   **Blacks (Urban Areas) Consolidation Act (No. 25 of 1945)**
The Committee recommends that participation in sport be excluded from the provisions of the Act through the amendment of Sections 9 and 10 of the Act.

Compiled by
Prof J C Van der Walt
Chairman of the Work Committee for the Jurisprudential Investigation into Sports Legislation

6. International Missions

White South African sports administrators, in collaboration with the Department of Information, have taken to inviting an increasing number of international sports personalities, administrators and parliamentarians to visit South Africa and 'to see for themselves'. The South Africans have not concealed the fact that they pay all expenses for such visits. Such expenses are nearly always adequately reimbursed—as far as the regime is concerned—by the favourable reports subsequently given of South Africa by the invitees. White South Africa is extremely careful to ensure that only persons who show some sympathy for its cause are invited.

On the other hand, persons who have openly condemned apartheid sport and wish to visit South Africa to support their claim that there is still widespread racial discrimination in sport have been refused entry into South Africa. Paul Stephenson, for example, a black member of the British Sports Council who rejected the conclusions reached by his Council in March 1980, on the issue of apartheid sport, thereupon announced that he would visit South Africa and table his own version. Stephenson applied for an entry permit in July 1980 and after much wrangling he was eventually notified in October 1980 that his application had 'not been successful.'[1]

In an appeal written directly to the South African Prime Minister shortly before this decision was reached, Stephenson had pointed out that to date, all his efforts to obtain an entry authorisation for South Africa had been 'impeded by political bureaucracy'. 'South Africa has always claimed that anyone who wished to visit the country "to see for themselves" the situation in South Africa was welcome to do so', the letter went on. 'But Paul Stephenson, a Black, who has made known his feelings on apartheid and racial discrimination, who holds a UK passport, must get special permission to visit South Africa.'[2]

In April 1981, in contrast, John Carlisle, a British Member of Parliament, had no great difficulty in gaining entry to South Africa. Carlisle, who had not concealed his sympathy for white South Africa, had been invited by South Africa's Department of Information. Both prior to and following his return Carlisle defended South Africa's 'multi-national' sports policy.

Fact-finding delegations

Although South Africa has been excluded from all major international sports competitions it nevertheless still has some influential friends within several international sports federations and other organisations. It has not hesitated to instigate a review of its sports situation through such friends, and since 1979, has managed to engineer visits to South Africa by several 'fact-finding delegations'. These have included delegations from the International Tennis Federation (1979), the International Cricket Conference (March 1979), a French Parliamentary Delegation (January 1980), and the British Sports Council (January 1980).

Black South Africans, the Supreme Council for Sport in Africa and the United Nations have always contended that no useful purpose will be served by sending any fact-finding mission to South Africa, and that such missions simply provide South Africa with a medium through which to appeal to the world to be allowed back into international sport.

Under the present political climate it is not possible for any commission, however objective it might profess to be, to give a full and true reflection of the South African sports situation. Blacks are either weary or afraid of expressing their opinions to international commissions because their opinions are always labelled 'lies' or 'anti-South African' by the regime, and because of the danger of their being victimised later. South Africa has ample legal machinery to deal with these 'offences'. When approached by such commissions, blacks therefore tend to either evade the question or feel obliged to praise the system; this 'praise' is then interpreted as an acceptance of the existing sports structure.

International commissions, in their desire to demonstrate their 'objectivity', usually wish to view both sides of the case—segregated and desegregated sport. Therefore the same amount of time tends to be spent on viewing the new-style 'multi-racial' sport as is devoted to viewing sports and facilities that are still segregated. Under the circumstances it is still very difficult to explain that integrated sport and integrated clubs constitute less than one per cent of the total sports activities in South Africa.[3] Consequently, such fact-finding delegations and commissions have tended to reinforce the impression that tremendous changes have occurred in South African sport.

Further, as these 'investigations' have often been engineered by South Africa in the first place the delegations are either heavily loaded in the regime's favour or are not in a position to take an independent line. The delegations from the British Sports Council and the International Tennis Federation, for example, followed the lines set by their respective leaders, both of whom displayed pro-apartheid views.

The British Sports Council

The British Sports Council's delegation was led by its chairman, Richard Jeeps. Despite the Sports Council's policy of dissuading British sportsmen and women from competing in South Africa he accepted an all-expenses paid trip to South Africa in April 1980,[4] to be the guest speaker at South Africa's Sports Greats Awards. Jeeps has also visited South Africa on a number of occasions to play and watch rugby with all-white teams.

Bernard Atha, Vice Chairman of the British Sports Council at the time of its mission to South Africa and a member of the delegation, said of its findings:

'There are many things about the report I am extremely unhappy about, particularly the unconscious bias in favour of the establishment. This will not serve the interests of South African sportsmen or the Sports Council.'[5]

At a press conference Jeeps stated that Basil D'Oliveira, another member of the Sports Council delegation, favoured the Lions rugby tour to South Africa. D'Oliveira later stated:

'I told Jeeps there is no way I can support the Lions' tour going to South Africa. I don't approve of the system in any way. I can't support any links whatever in sport or any other way with South Africa while the present system exists. How the hell can you divorce sport and politics? I'm coloured and you are white and we can play together, but we can't drink together after the game, or eat at the same restaurant. Life and sport are inextricably entwined. The system must be broken down. Sporting isolation was brought about because of the system. The system hasn't changed and so why should the links be re-established?'.[6]

The International Tennis Federation

Phillipe Chatrier, President of the International Tennis Federation (ITF), and leader of the ITF's mission to South Africa in 1979, said on his return:

'Every year I go to South Africa to examine the sports situation in that country and I can confirm that, with regard to tennis, the barriers are tumbling one by one, leading to total non-discrimination. That is the way I see it. People I speak to here and in South Africa are stating clearly now that they do not wish to practise sport under any circumstances whatsoever, non-racial or otherwise, until apartheid as a political system has been completely abolished. Now we are beginning to understand. It is clear we are not speaking about the same thing. I as a sports administrator can only concern myself with apartheid in sport and there is none in South Africa as far as tennis is concerned. I shall explain this to the general assembly of tennis administrators. Moreover I think that this sport can only bring the communities closer to each other, it can only do good and lead to another step towards the abolition of apartheid which we all want.'[7]

During 1981 Chatrier paid further compliments to white South Africa, while criticising black tennis players for obstructing reform:

'I feel that the South African Tennis Union has done everything possible within the laws of their country even to the point of having some of those laws changed to make a completely non-racial game a reality. It has not worked for this simple reason: The leaders of Non-White tennis, who, when we first went to South Africa had a slogan 'Can we play normal sport in an abnormal society?' were saying openly during our second visit that they were not prepared to allow tennis (or any integrated sport) to take place in that abnormal society. They say that tennis is only a small part of life and they are prepared to sacrifice it to fulfil their main aim. The second delegation was asked to apportion the blame for the lack of progress towards a unified tennis federation, which everyone would be happy to join and share in the competition and administration.

We left Johannesburg after another round of long discussions without any hope that this would materialise in the forseeable future because the Non-White tennis unions had hardened their attitude and had rejected all SATU's invitations to begin negotiations for a new body. As far as tennis is concerned, the blame for this lack of progress must lie with the Non-White associations.'[8]

The anti-apartheid Tennis Association of South Africa (TASA) replied to these criticisms in a lengthy letter to Chatrier dated 11 November 1981. TASA stated *inter alia*:

'A few years ago SATU claimed in a glossy (*à la* INFORMATION) brochure that 'sport in South Africa is non-racial'. In it there were quite a few pictures showing tennis coaching. Any careful observer would have noticed that the same group of people was photographed from different angles, and that the young people all happen to be of the same 'race'. An unbiased observer would have agreed with the statement of the Minister of Sport at that time that such 'happenings' represented only 0.05% of all sport. In other words: 'normal' sport is not normal.

'You had the opportunity of visiting Umlazi, Kwa Mashu (remember, you needed a permit to do so) and you saw the facilities there. You have seen how these difficulties (*sic*) are not being used as they should, because people have to travel between 60 and 80 kilometres per day in order to make a living, and are debarred from using any facilities in the area where they work. You will admit that you have not seen a single situation which can be construed as an example of integration, except, perhaps, in the office where permits are issued.

'Mr Chatrier, except for one case in Cape Town when someone you would refer to as 'non-white' emerged from a shower room, what other examples of integration have you noticed in tennis?

'We really do not know which of these laws have been changed, what we do know is that the responsible Minister, just prior to your annual congress and those of other international controlling bodies, promised to have these changes effected in the near future. What we also do know is that during the last few years some provisions of certain statutes were not applied—that certain transgressions of the laws were allowed in respect of sport. But, surely, everybody knows that the non-application of a law in no way makes it ineffective. In South Africa certain legal measures dating from the last century have, as recently as the latter quarter of this one, been used for prosecutions.

'What the Minister envisages to do, is to amend certain laws so that they do not apply to the sports scene. You are under a serious misapprehension if you believe that the sports scene will be changed at all by the proposed amendments to the Urban Areas, Group Areas and Liquor Acts. The scenario for 1982 will not differ at all from that which you have observed during all your previous visits.

'If as your statement implies, SATU was responsible for having the above three laws changed then they must stand accused of being accessories in the exercise of delusion which is now being inflicted upon the international community. The fact of the matter is that most of the restrictions that will be lifted in due course are ENTRENCHED in the lesser known, but more vicious Separate Amenities Act. Moreover the statute that is basic to the whole system of Sportsapartheid—the Population Registration Act—is considered to be immutable and non-negotiable. And equally important, the institutions that were spawned by the Apartheid ideology, for example separate residential areas, and separate education are to be retained *in toto*.

'The architects of Apartheid and so, too, those who exploit Sportsapartheid for material gain, all claim that sport in South Africa is in the process of being normalised and depoliticised.

'Insofar as these claims are concerned we, the victims of Sportsapartheid, know that is not the case. The removal of certain statutory restrictions and the retention of other, equally vicious statutory measures AND institutions in no way address the fundamental problem. It is the height of absurdity to believe that we can have normal sport when we cannot lead normal LIVES.'

The International Cricket Conference
In July 1978 some members of the International Cricket Conference (ICC), despite opposition by the West Indies, India and Pakistan, accepted an invitation to examine the position of cricket in South Africa. It is not known who paid for the travelling and other expenses of the delegation. The delegation was, with the exception of Alma Hunt of Bermuda, exclusively white.

The success of the South African government in deceiving the outside world was adequately substantiated in the unofficial ICC report of the visit. The delegation found that
'Whatever the statute books may say, there is little evidence of separate development in all its manifestations to the ordinary visitor in the major cities. In shops and banks coloured people work side by side and customers of all races patronise the establishments.'
The report went on to say that
'there was ample evidence during our travels that entirely integrated cricket does exist and is played on a regular basis at club and provincial

level. Both before, during and after these cricket matches all players were able to participate equally in the facilities offered.'

The delegation concluded

'In our opinion the South African Cricket Union (SACU) is a body representative of the majority of cricketers in South Africa and as far as the ICC is concerned should be recognised as the governing body of cricket in South Africa.

'The commission recommends that, subject to an invitation being received, a strong team, representative of as many countries as possible, from ICC be sent to play a series of matches at the highest representative level during the 1979/80 season.'[9]

At the 1980 meeting of the ICC a motion apparently tabled by England and supported by New Zealand recommending the acceptance of South Africa (SACU) was withdrawn because of lack of support.

Although overseas blacks are given 'honorary white' status during their stay in South Africa it was later revealed that this dispensation could not apply in South Africa's white parliament. Permission to entertain members of the unofficial ICC delegation in the parliamentary dining-room was refused because the invitees contained blacks, Alma Hunt (ICC delegation) and Rashid Varachia (president of SACU).[10]

An epic legal case - SACU forced to withdraw
The anti-apartheid South African Council on Sport (SACOS) and its affiliates have always maintained that the South African Cricket Union (SACU) is a government-recognised organisation which, like all the other government-recognised sports bodies, administers sport within the framwork of apartheid sports policy, thereby practising 'multi-nationalism' as opposed to non-racialism. SACU contested this claim twice in the South African Supreme Court but twice felt obliged to withdraw the charges against SACOS and to elect to pay all costs.

SACOS was looking forward to contesting, in the highest South African courts, SACU's claim to be operating a 'normal' cricket set-up. If successful SACOS would have proved, once and for all, that non-racial sport was not possible in racially structured South Africa.

The case would have made legal history in South Africa. However it is safe to say that SACU's recognition of the weakness of its own arguments was the main factor prompting its leadership to settle out of court.

Documents IX and X explain the sequence of events leading eventually to SACU agreeing to pay all SACOS's costs.

Document IX: Writ issued by the South African Cricket Union against the South African Council on Sport

IN THE SUPREME COURT OF SOUTH AFRICA
DURBAN AND COAST LOCAL DIVISION

In the matter between:

THE SOUTH AFRICAN CRICKET UNION   Plaintiff

and

THE SOUTH AFRICAN COUNCIL OF SPORT (*sic*)   Defendant

To:	The Sheriff or his Deputy:
INFORM	THE SOUTH AFRICAN COUNCIL OF SPORT, an unincorporated body of persons not being a partnership, an association as is envisaged in terms of Rule 14(1) of the Rules of the Supreme Court of South Africa, of Suite 203, Victoria Heights, 56/8 Victoria Street, Durban, being its place of business, *alternatively* of care of HASSAN HOWA the chairman or the secretary of the committee of the Defendant of P.O. Box 2451, Durban, 4000, (hereinafter called the Defendant).
that	THE SOUTH AFRICAN CRICKET UNION, an association not for gain incorporated as a company limited by guarantee in terms of the law of the Republic of South Africa with its registered office at The Oval, Wanderers' Grounds, Corlett Drive, Illovo, Johannesburg, (hereinafter called the Plaintiff),

hereby institutes action against it in which action the Plaintiff claims the relief and on the grounds set out in the particulars annexed hereto.

INFORM	the defendant further that if it disputes the claim and wishes to defend the action it shall:-
(i)	within TEN (10) days of the service upon it of this Summons file with the Registrar of this Court at Supreme Court Buildings, Victoria Embankment, Durban, notice of its intention to defend and serve a copy thereof on the Plaintiff's Attorneys, which notice shall give an address (not being a post office box or poste restante) referred to in Rule 6 (5) (b) for the service upon the Defendant of all notices and documents in the action; such an address is one within eight kilometres of the office of the Registrar, or, if the Defendant in person or his attorney is a person who is in terms of any law prohibited from being the occupier of land or premises within the distance of eight kilometres of such office, an address further than eight kilometres from such office but within the magisterial district in which such office is situated;
(ii)	thereafter, and within TWENTY-ONE days after filing and serving notice of intention to defend as aforesaid, file with the Registrar and serve upon the Plaintiff a Plea, exception, notice to strike out, with or without a counter-claim.

INFORM   the Defendant further that if it fails to file and serve notice as aforesaid, Judgment as claimed may be given against it without further notice to it, or if, having filed and served such notice, it fails to plead, except, make application to strike out, or counter-claim, Judgment may be given against it.

AND IMMEDIATELY   thereafter serve on the Defendant a copy of this Summons and return the same to the Registrar with whatsoever you have done thereupon.

DATED at DURBAN this 17th day of JULY, 1978.

REGISTRAR OF THE SUPREME COURT

EDWARD NATHAN & FRIEDLAND INC.,
Plaintiff's Attorneys,
5th Floor, Innes Chambers,
Pritchard Street,
JOHANNESBURG.

c/o WARTSKI, GREENBURG,
4th Floor, Trust Bank Centre,
475 Smith Street,
DURBAN.

ANNEXURE

PARTICULARS OF PLAINTIFF'S CLAIM

1. The Plaintiff is THE SOUTH AFRICAN CRICKET UNION, an association not for gain incorporated as a company limited by guarantee in terms of the laws of the Republic of South Africa with its registered offices at The Oval, Wanderers' Grounds, Corlett Drive, Illovo, Johannesburg.

2. The Defendant is THE SOUTH AFRICAN COUNCIL OF SPORT, an unincorporated body of persons not being a partnership, an association as is envisaged in terms of Rule 14(1) of the Rules of the Supreme Court of South Africa, of Suite 203, Victoria Heights, 56/8 Victoria Street, Durban, being its place of business, *alternatively* of care of HASSAN HOWA the chairman or the secretary of the committee of the Defendant of P.O. Box 2451, Durban, 4000.

3. (a) During the period 1977 and 1978 and throughout the Republic of South Africa the Defendant addressed and published to its members and associates and to the public at large a written document wherein the Defendant wrongfully, unlawfully and maliciously wrote the following words of and concerning the Plaintiff:

> "All clubs, unions, associations, leagues, boards and federations which are members of non-racial, national or provincial bodies are duty bound to implement the following resolution of the South African Council of Sport:
>
> No person, whether he is a player, an administrator or a spectator, committed to the non-racial principle in sport, shall participate in or be associated with any code of sport which practise, perpetuate or condone racialism or multinationalism. Players and/or administrators disregarding the essence of this principle shall be guilty of practising double standards, and cannot therefore, be members of any organisation affiliated to SACOS."

(b) The defendant furthermore included the name of the Plaintiff in a list of persons which it addressed and published in conjunction with the document referred to in sub-paragraph (a) above as being persons which practise,

57

perpetuate or condone racialism or multi-nationalism in sport.

4.   (a)   The said words were intended by the Defendant and were understood by the various persons to whom the said words were addressed and published to mean that the Plaintiff, its committee and its members were persons who, inter alia, practise racialism, alternatively practise multi-nationalism which was equated by the Defendant with racialism and as such were persons unfit to administer, manage or control cricketing activities in the Republic of South Africa.

    (b)   *Alternatively to (a):*
The Plaintiff was at all material times hereto, and to the knowledge of the Defendant and to the knowledge of the various persons to whom the said words were addressed and published, administrators of sport in the Republic of South Africa, and the said words were intended by the Defendant and understood by the aforementioned persons to mean that the Plaintiff, its committee and its members, were not persons to be entrusted with the administration of Sport in the Republic of South Africa, and were persons unfit to administer, manage or control cricketing activities in the Republic of South Africa.

5.   By the use of the aforesaid words the Defendant has caused the Plaintiff damage in the sum of R15 000-00

6.   *Alternatively to paragraphs 4 and 5 above:*

    (a)   The said words were untrue of the plaintiff and by reason thereof the Plaintiff has suffered injury in that:

        (i)   its good name and reputation have been injured;

        (ii)   potential members of the Plaintiff have been influenced in consequence to refrain from becoming members of the Plaintiff;

        (iii)   the Plaintiff's name, standing and goodwill both in the Republic of South Africa, and elsewhere have been injured;

    thereby causing loss to the Plaintiff.

    (b)   By reason of the publication of the aforesaid false statements of and concerning the Plaintiff, the latter has suffered damages in the sum of R15 000-00.

7.   The Defendant is wrongfully, unlawfully and maliciously persisting in such publication as aforesaid, causing the Plaintiff further damages as aforesaid, and in the premises the Plaintiff is entitled to an order interdicting the Defendant from continuing to publish the said words.

WHEREFORE the Plaintiff claims:

1.   (a)   Payment of the sum of R15 000 as damages as aforesaid.

    (b)   Interest on the said sum of R15 000 at a rate of 11% per annum from date of judgment to date of payment.

	(c)	Further or alternative relief.

(d) Cost of suit.

2. (a) An order interdicting the Defendant from publishing the words referred to in paragraph 3 of the Plaintiff's particulars of claim with reference to the Plaintiff.

(b) Further or alternative relief.

(c) Cost of suit.

DATED AT JOHANNESBURG this 6th day of JULY, 1978.

R J GOLDSTONE

D BREGMAN
Counsel for the Plaintiff

EDWARD NATHAN AND FRIEDLAND INC.
Plaintiff's Attorneys
5th Floor Innes Chamber,
Pritchard Street,
JOHANNESBURG.

c/o WARTSKI, GREENBURG,
4th Floor, Trust Bank Centre,
475 Smith Street,
DURBAN.

Document X: SACU's Notice of Withdrawal

IN THE SUPREME COURT OF SOUTH AFRICA
DURBAN AND COAST LOCAL DIVISION   CASE NO: I.2569/1978

In the matter between:

THE SOUTH AFRICAN CRICKET UNION   Plaintiff

and

THE SOUTH AFRICAN COUNCIL OF SPORT (*sic*)   Defendant

NOTICE OF WITHDRAWAL

TO: THE REGISTRAR OF THE SUPREME COURT
             DURBAN

AND TO: PAUL DAVID & COMPANY
             Defendant's Attorneys
             c/o YUNUS MAHOMED & ASSOCIATES
             formerly Shun Chetty & Co
             602 Teachers Centre
             113 Albert Street
             DURBAN

SIRS,
KINDLY TAKE NOTICE that the Plaintiff hereby withdraws the above Action and Tenders to
pay the Defendant's Taxed or Agreed costs to date.

DATED at DURBAN this 17th day of JANUARY 1980.

EDWARD NATHAN AND FRIEDLAND INC.
c/o WARTSKI, GREENBURG,
Plaintiff's Attorneys
4th Floor, Trust Bank Centre,
475 Smith Street,
DURBAN.

7. The Boycott Weapon

From the 1950s onwards, a large body of evidence was accumulated of racial discrimination in South African sport. This did not, however, lead automatically to the regime's expulsion from international sport. Various blocking devices by western countries, traditional supporters of white South Africa, protected South African affiliations to international sports federations and its participation in international events.

In the face of the failure to enforce effective sporting sanctions against South Africa, African, other Third World and Socialist countries began to be reluctantly compelled to use the boycott weapon directly themselves to keep South Africa out of international sport. In 1968 the threat of a boycott of the Mexico Olympics forced the International Olympic Committee to exclude South Africa. South Africa was eventually expelled from the Olympic movement altogether in 1970.

Similarly, in 1972, the Africans effected the exclusion of what was then Rhodesia from the Munich Olympic Games. Third World and Socialist countries subsequently forced South Africa out of many international events by indicating that they would withdraw if South Africa was allowed to participate.

In 1976 nineteen African countries, Guyana and Iraq took the unprecedented step of implementing their threat of a boycott of the Montreal Olympic Games, in protest against New Zealand sending its national rugby team to South Africa. Many other countries have since made it known that such obvious collusion with South African sport will not be tolerated and that they will reconsider their participation in sports events together with such collaborators.

The boycott of the 1976 Montreal Olympic Games forced many western countries to re-examine their attitude towards apartheid sport. Canada, which suffered badly by the Olympic boycott of 1976, was determined that its 1978 Edmonton Commonwealth Games would not be affected by another boycott.

The Commonwealth Heads of Government, meeting in London in June 1977, were obliged, for the first time, to give special consideration to the problem of apartheid sport, especially the effects it would have on the Edmonton Commonwealth Games if Commonwealth countries persisted in maintaining sports exchanges with South Africa.

On 15 June 1977 the Commonwealth countries issued the *Commonwealth Statement on Apartheid in Sport* (popularly known as the Gleneagles

Agreement) which stated, *inter alia,* that:

'Heads of Government specially welcomed the belief, unanimously expressed at their Meeting, that in the light of their consultations and accord there were unlikely to be future sporting contacts of any significance between Commonwealth countries or their nationals and South Africa while that country continues to pursue the detestable policy of apartheid. On that basis, and having regard to their commitments, they look foward with satisfaction to the holding of the Commonwealth Games in Edmonton and to the continued strengthening of Commonwealth sport generally.'

The statement was adopted unanimously by the Commonwealth countries *(The full text of the Gleneagles Agreement is reproduced in Document XI).*

In December 1977 the General Assembly of the United Nations also adopted a declaration to isolate South Africa from international sport. *The International Declaration Against Apartheid in Sports* called on all member countries to cease all sports exchanges with South Africa. *(See full text in Document XII).*

Since the adoption of the Gleneagles Agreement in 1977 Commonwealth countries have intensified their campaign to isolate apartheid sport. Only two countries, New Zealand and the United Kingdom, have so far refused to directly intervene to stop their nationals and teams from maintaining sports links with South Africa.

South Africa has responded to the international campaign to isolate apartheid sport by offering huge financial rewards to international sports stars to persuade them to compete in South Africa. Astronomical sums of money are being expended to effect collaboration. In doing so South Africa is precipitating the use of the boycott weapon by other countries and thereby provoking disruption of international sport.

South Africa is hoping that such disruption will lead to division between the western countries and the Third World and socialist countries. The regime apparently expects that such division will allow it to resume sports contacts with its traditional allies in the west and elsewhere. The pro-South African lobby within the western countries, for its part, is facilitating collaboration with apartheid sport. Furthermore, by creating this uncertain international atmosphere, South Africa is anticipating striking some form of deal with the International Olympic Committee and other international sports federations.

White South Africa always welcomes any visit by overseas sportsmen as a form of support of the apartheid system. Sportsmen and women who defy international appeals not to play in South Africa are hailed as 'our friends' by the whites.

This is clear in statements from the South African government too:

'Although it is true that there was no competition in the main types of sport, there is nevertheless proof that South Africa still has many sports friends and that sportsmen from abroad still wish to compete against us'.[1]

'In the year under review, from 1 October 1978 to 30 September 1979, we can look up how many sportsmen visited South Africa from Western countries and practised their sport here. Sport is a wonderful catalyst which brings peoples of various international convictions together and makes them forget their differences in the challenge of the sport. We must not relegate sport to a insignificant component of our international counter-offensive, but South Africa should rather use the platform that sport offers in order to build bridges between nations.'[2]

In recent years, the South African government and its recognised sports establishment have begun actively to promote sports not (as at the time of writing) directly affected by isolation. In addition to the regular golf, tennis and other tournaments in which professionals from all over the world continue to participate as a matter of routine, the South African sports establishment has organised several spectacular events which visibly evade sanctions. In 1979 and 1980, for example, the World Boxing Association (WBA) World Heavyweight Boxing Championships were staged in South Africa, and in 1980 an attempt was made to arrange a 'super-match' between tennis stars Bjorn Borg and John McEnroe. The tennis match, had it not been aborted, would have been sport's biggest moneyspinner outside professional boxing *(see Chapter 8)*.

The problems posed by sportsmen who choose to contravene the general rules of their international or national bodies against contact with South Africa have become acute for another reason. South Africans have become adept at breaking isolation by deception. For instance, individual footballers and cricketers have been assembled in South Africa for matches against South African teams. The international sports federations and national governments both have cause to be concerned at the spread of this kind of deception, which flouts decisions made by the responsible authorities of the federations or governments themselves.

Since the late 1970s, South Africa has initiated a major offensive to break out of its sport isolation, which has been by and large concentrated on three major international sports, *viz,* rugby, cricket and football.

The rugby conspiracy
The major international rugby playing countries belong to the International Rugby Board (IRB). This is made up of England, Wales, Scotland, Ireland, France, New Zealand, Australia and South Africa. All members of the IRB have strongly supported the white South African Rugby Board and have resisted all moves to terminate rugby exchanges with South Africa.

The South Africans, fully conscious of the support of the IRB, have used rugby as a battering ram to break out of their international sports isolation.

In 1980, in particular, South Africa entertained the French national side and the combined British and Irish teams (the Lions). In October 1980 the South Africans toured South America (Chile, Uruguay and Paraguay—the

Argentinian government refused the team members visas). In rugby-playing terms the South American tour was most insignificant but, nevertheless, South Africa made great political propoganda of it. It stated that it had played three 'Tests' and that it had re-established all its international links. In 1981 the Irish national team toured South Africa and the South Africans toured New Zealand and the USA.

The New Zealand government's refusal in 1976 to intervene to stop its rugby team touring South Africa prompted many countries to boycott the 1976 Montreal Olympic Games. The government maintained its stand in 1981 by permitting the South African Springbok rugby team to tour New Zealand.

This decision led to worldwide condemnation of both the government and the New Zealand rugby authorities. Anti-apartheid groups in New Zealand mobilised to hold large demonstrations at all the tour's match venues. The New Zealand government responded by voting over $2 million for police reinforcements to control the demonstrators.

Commonwealth countries protested at New Zealand's insistence on proceeding with the tour by moving the Commonwealth Finance Ministers' Conference from Auckland to Nassau in the Bahamas.

Massive demonstrations preceded every match of the tour. Two matches had to be cancelled but still the New Zealand government and its rugby authorities persevered with their plans. The police assaulted the demonstrators, many of whom were badly injured. About a thousand demonstrators were charged for various offences.

The South African Rugby Board (SARB), wishing to display its appreciation to New Zealand, invited members of the New Zealand police for a short tour of South Africa. This offer was refused and the SARB instead gave consideration to the idea of donating money for a police holiday home in New Zealand.

The USA leg of the South Africans' 1981 rugby tour was conducted in secret because of the fear of anti-apartheid demonstrations. It was organised by the Eastern Rugby Union (ERU) in the United States. Louis Luyt, the South African businessman who had been involved in the secret operations of the South African Ministry of Information during the 'Muldergate scandal', gave the Eastern Rugby Union $25,000 prior to ERU's invitation to the Springboks to play in the United States.[3]

The South African Rugby Board secretly gave the ERU another $50,000 in connection with the tour.[4]

The number of rugby internationals played by South Africa in the last few years is a record for any country and the number of exchanges recorded by South Africa during this period is unprecedented. They were all engineered specifically to provoke a major international sports crisis, which would work to the benefit of apartheid sports.

The rebel English cricket tour

South Africa's application for membership of the International Cricket Conference (ICC) has been repeatedly blocked by the powerful black cricketing nations of India, Pakistan and the West Indies.

Unable to impress the ICC by veneering over its apartheid sports policy, South Africa decided to provoke an international cricket furore by offering extraordinarily large sums of money to some English cricketers who would be assembled in South Africa as an English international cricket team.

In March 1982 twelve England cricketers secretly landed in South Africa for a six week tour, the whole of which was underwritten by the South African Breweries. Each player was said to have received £50,000.[5]

It was widely reported that Geoff Boycott, the English international cricketer from Yorkshire, was largely responsible for recruiting players for the tour. One of the recruited players, Dennis Amiss, agreed that the cash was 'too good to ignore'.[6] Altogether, fifteen English cricketers took part in this pirate venture.

As soon as the tour was announced India, Pakistan and the West Indies made it known that this would complicate their future cricket relations with England. India and Pakistan indicated that they would refuse to play against any of the cricketers who participated in the unofficial South African tour during their own forthcoming tours of England.

In South Africa itself the tour was a flop, with little spectator interest in the matches. Nevertheless, South Africa once again boasted that it had broken the international sports isolation barrier.

Not all cricketers who had been approached accepted the huge cash offers to play in South Africa. Ian Botham, a star English cricketer, refused to play in South Africa. The South Africans still persevered and came back with a virtual 'name your own price' offer to Botham. Botham's reply was that he wouldn't go 'even if they offered me the moon'.[7]

With the threat of India and Pakistan refusing to tour England if no sanctions were imposed on the rebel cricketers, and the consequent loss of an estimated £2 million in gate and television revenue, the English Test and County Cricket Board was reluctantly forced to announce some action. On 19 March 1982 the English cricket authorities announced that all fifteen who had taken part in the unofficial cricket tour of South Africa were banned from representing England for the next three years. The English County Clubs also agreed that none of the fifteen would play in games against the Indian and Pakistan tourists. Furthermore, the English Test and County Cricket Board warned that there would be no Test place for any player who in future went to South Africa on a similar tour.

The sanction busting football tour of July 1982

Later in 1982, realising the potential for attracting top quality sportsmen and women with sufficiently inflated appearance fees, South Africa embarked on yet another venture to break out of isolation. The South African Breweries again emerged as the benefactor of apartheid sport by underwriting an international football tour of South Africa for a record £1 million.[8]

As football is by and large played and watched in South Africa by blacks the regime apparently hoped that there would be much more international sympathy for this tour than for others such as that by the cricketers a few months previously. This whole venture was initiated on the basis of deceit. After a London Sunday newspaper had revealed that a secret football tour of South Africa was planned South Africa's football officials—both black and white—confessed that they knew nothing about the proposed tour.

Only after the arrangements had been made did South Africa's football administrators officially hear about it. It was evident that the tour had been planned by people who wished to gain political mileage for South Africa, otherwise the tour would have been planned in consultation with football administrators. Further, it is possible that there was direct South African government involvement in this project.

The project was, nevertheless, doomed to fail right from the beginning. In contrast with the circumstances of the earlier cricket tour, the rules of the International Football Federation (FIFA) specifically state that there cannot be match contact between member and non-member countries of FIFA. South Africa was expelled from FIFA in 1976 for practising racial discrimination. Despite this, Jimmy Hill, a BBC television sports presenter and the chairman of an English football league club, Coventry City, who acted as consultant for the tour, left the prospective players with the impression that he had discovered a legal loophole which would enable them to avoid an international ban.

Kevin Keegan, the English football captain, was offered £250,000 to play in the six-match tour.[9] Another footballer, Justin Fashanu, was offered a figure believed to be as much as £200,000.[10] Both players turned down the offers.

Two Argentinian World Cup Stars, Osvaldo Ardiles and Mario Kempes, arrived in South Africa but left without having played a match because they feared FIFA sanctions. Dirceu, a Bazilian world cup star, also withdrew on learning that he would be subjected to FIFA sanctions.

Other internationals including Johan Cruyff from Holland and Franz Beckenbauer of West Germany were approached but it is thought that they were dissuaded.[11]

The whole affair was brought to the attention of FIFA by the African Football Confederation (CAF) during the FIFA Congress held in Madrid in early July 1982.

To try and give this tour as much international respectability as possible the organisers even recruited overseas referees for the matches. Jack Taylor, an English referee, accompanied the tour party to South Africa but Clive Thomas, one of Britain's best referees, turned down an offer of £10,000.[12] Thomas, a 46 year-old Welshman, said:

'I would have earned more there in three weeks than in the next two years in the (English) Football League, but for me it wasn't a question of money but principle. I don't agree with what's going on in South Africa'.[13]

The team which finally emerged was British with the exception of Franz Von Bastijns of Belgium.[14] All the players were either past their prime or well short of stardom.

When the team assembled in South Africa black anti-apartheid groups mobilised their forces to ensure that black resistance to this plan to provide apartheid with respectability was clearly apparent. Three of South Africa's top black teams, Kaiser Chiefs, Orlando Pirates and Moroka Swallows, refused to play the so-called international team.

After having fulfilled only two of the fixtures in nearly empty football grounds the organisers had to concede defeat. The tour was terminated after only three of the scheduled six matches had been played. The premature termination of the tour, unprecedented in South African sports history, heralded a new epoch in the sports resistance movement. Never before had resistance inside South Africa led to the total collapse of a sports tour.

This failed project will, it is hoped, finally make South Africa realise that salvation in international sport will only come from the abandonment of apartheid and not from constantly sugar-coating the apartheid sports structure or from offers of astronomical sums of money to sports stars.

Counter-reaction—Freedom in Sport (FIS)

The growing success of the international sports boycott of South Africa has in turn prompted a series of counter-moves by the regime's sympathisers abroad. These have taken the form, in particular, of concerted drives to win favourable publicity for South Africa and South African sport in the world's press and media, culminating in the establishment of specific organisations dedicated to advancing the South African cause.

Britain, where the boycott campaign has a history of more than two decades, has been the cradle for a number of such pro-apartheid propaganda bodies. In the sports field, one of the most recent has been the Freedom in Sport (FIS) campaign. Freedom in Sport was formed in London in June 1981 with the apparent aims:

a. To promote non-racial sport.
b. To encourage international participation in all individual and team sports.
c. To assist participation in sport free from interference or influence by Government of any other organisation or individual.

Although this organisation's aims might seem sound and innocent, in practice, it concentrated all its efforts in aiding South Africa to break out of its

67

sports isolation. This was not surprising in view of the established reputation of several of its officials for lobbying for the re-admission of South Africa into international sport.

From its inception, FIS supported all international sports links and exchanges with apartheid South Africa. One of its members even travelled to Australia for the 1981 Commonwealth Conference to lobby for the scrapping of the Gleneagles Agreement.[15] FIS did not seem to have received any favourable response from Commonwealth leaders. It is believed that the FIS representations were largely ignored.

The efforts of FIS in lobbying on behalf of South African sport nevertheless began to pay dividends. In December 1981 for example the South African Rugby Board announced that it would give R20,000 to FIS. It was planned to pay the R20,000 in R5,000 instalments 'as they need it'.[16]

Commenting on FIS at the time of its launch in London, the *Observer* newspaper remarked that:

> 'We recall that a few years ago a similar-sounding organisation, called the Committee for Fairness in Sport, set itself up in South Africa with the very same ideals—to promote freedom of choice and so-called multi-racialism. Let us hope the similarities end there for that entirely 'non-political organisation' turned out to be financed by the government slush fund which helped to bring down the Prime Minister Vorster.'[17]

Document XI: Text of the Commonwealth Statement on Apartheid in Sport

(Adopted at the Commonwealth Summit Meeting in London on 15 June 1977 and generally known as the Gleneagles Agreement)

The member countries of the Commonwealth, embracing peoples of diverse races, colours, languages and faiths, have long recognised racial prejudice and discrimination as a dangerous sickness and an unmitigated evil and are pledged to use all their efforts to foster human dignity everywhere. At their London Meeting, Heads of Government reaffirmed that apartheid in sports, as in other fields, is an abomination and runs directly counter to the Declaration of Commonwealth Principles which they made at Singapore on 22 January 1971.

They were conscious that sport is an important means of developing and fostering understanding between the people, and especially between the young people of all countries. But, they were also aware that, quite apart from other factors, sporting contacts between their nationals and the nationals of countries practising apartheid in sport tend to encourage the belief (however unwarranted) that they are prepared to condone this abhorrent policy or are less than totally committed to the Principles embodied in their Singapore Declaration. Regretting past misunderstandings and difficulties and recognising that these were partly the result of inadequate inter-governmental consultations, they agreed that they would seek to remedy this situation in the context of the increased level of understanding now achieved.

They reaffirmed their full support for the international campaign against apartheid and welcomed the efforts of the United Nations to reach universally accepted approaches to the question of sporting contacts within the framework of that campaign.

Mindful of these and other considerations, they accepted it as the urgent duty of each of their Governments vigorously to combat the evil of apartheid by withholding any form of support for, and by taking every practical step to discourage contact or competition by their nationals with sporting organisations, teams or sportsmen from South Africa or from any other country where sports are organised on the basis of race, colour or ethnic origin.

They fully acknowledged that it was for each Government to determine in accordance with its laws the methods by which it might best discharge these commitments. But they recognised that the effective fulfilment of their commitments was essential to the harmonious development of Commonwealth sport hereafter.

They acknowledged also that the full realisation of their objectives involved the understanding, support and active participation of the nationals of their countries and of their national sporting organisations and authorities. As they drew a curtain across the past they issued a collective call for that understanding, support and participation with a view to ensuring that in this matter the peoples and Governments of the Commonwealth might help to give a lead to the world.

Heads of Government specially welcomed the belief, unanimously expressed at their Meeting, that in the light of their consultations and accord there were unlikely to be future sporting contacts of any significance between Commonwealth countries or their nationals and South Africa while that country continues to pursue the detestable policy of apartheid. On that basis, and having regard to their commitments, they looked forward with satisfaction to the holding of the Commonwealth Games in Edmonton and to the continued strengthening of Commonwealth sport generally.

London, June 15, 1977

Document XII: Text of the International Declaration Against Apartheid in Sports

(Adopted by the United Nations General Assembly on 14 December 1977)

The General Assembly,

Recalling its resolution 31/6 F of 9 November 1976 on *apartheid* in sports,

Reaffirming the importance of effective international action to abolish *apartheid* in sports and in all other fields,

Having considered the report of the *Ad Hoc* Committee on the Drafting of an International Convention against *Apartheid* in Sports,

1. *Adopts and proclaims* the International Declaration against *Apartheid* in Sports, recommended by the *Ad Hoc* Committee on the Drafting of an International Convention against *Apartheid* in Sports and annexed to the present resolution;

2. *Requests* the *Ad Hoc* Committee to draft an international convention against *apartheid* in sports for submission to the General Assembly at its thirty-third session;

3. *Authorizes* the *Ad Hoc* Committee to consult with representatives of organizations concerned and experts on *apartheid* in sports;

4. *Decides* that summary records should be be provided for meetings of the *Ad Hoc* Committee;

5. *Requests* the Secretary-General to provide all necessary assistance to the *Ad Hoc* Committee in the discharge of its task.

14 December 1977

Annex: International Declaration against *Apartheid* in Sports

The General Assembly,

Recalling the provisions of the Charter of the United Nations, in which Member States pledge to take joint and separate action in co-operation with the Organization for the achievement of universal respect for and observance of human rights and fundamental freedoms for all without distinction as to race, sex, language or religion,

Considering the Universal Declaration of Human Rights, which states that all humans beings are born free and equal in dignity and rights and that everyone is entitled to all the rights and freedoms set forth in the Declaration without distinction of any kind such as race, colour or national origin,

Recalling that, in accordance with the principles of the International Convention on the Elimination of All Forms of Racial Discrimination, States undertake not to sponsor, defend or support racial discrimination,

Recalling further that the International Convention on the Suppression and Punishment of the Crime of *Apartheid* declares that *apartheid* is a crime violating the principles of international law, in particular the purposes and principles of the Charter of the United Nations, and constituting a serious threat to international peace and security,

Noting that the General Assembly of the United Nations has adopted a number of resolutions in which the policies and practices of *apartheid*, including the application of *apartheid* in the field of sport, and collaboration with the racist régime in all areas, are condemned,

Reaffirming the legitimacy of the struggle of the people of South Africa for the total elimination of *apartheid* and racial discrimination,

Recognizing that the eradication of *apartheid* and rendering of assistance to the South African people to establish a non-racial society is one of the primary concerns of the international community,

Convinced that more effective measures must be taken as a matter of priority, during the International Anti-*Apartheid* Year and the Decade to Combat Racism and Racial Discrimination to eliminate *apartheid* in all its manifestations,

Reaffirming its unqualified support for the Olympic principle that no discrimination be allowed on the grounds of race, religion or political affiliation and its belief that merit should be the sole criterion for participation in sports activities,

Considering that international representative sporting contacts based on the Olympic principle can play a positive role in promoting peace and the development of friendly relations among nations of the world,

Recognizing that there can be neither adherence to the principle of merit selection nor fully integrated non-racial sport in any country practising *apartheid* until the *apartheid* system itself is eradicated,

Condemning the enforcement, by the racist régime of South Africa, of racial discrimination and segregation in sports,

Commending the sportsmen inside South Africa who are struggling against *apartheid* and upholding the principle of non-racialism in sport,

Condemning the represssive measures taken by the racist *apartheid* régime against the non-racial sports bodies and their leaders in South Africa,

Rejecting the policy of so-called 'multi-national' sport, enunciated by the South African racist régime, as no more than a device for perpetuating *apartheid* in sports and an attempt by the régime to mislead international public opinion in order to gain acceptance for participation in international sport,

Recognizing the importance in the international campaign against *apartheid* of the boycott of South African sports teams selected on the basis of *apartheid*,

Convinced that an effective campaign for the total boycott of South African sports teams can be an important measure in demonstrating the abhorrence of *apartheid* by Governments and peoples,

Commending all Governments, sportsmen, sports bodies and other organizations which have taken action against *apartheid* in sports,

Noting with concern that some national and international sports bodies have continued contacts with racist *apartheid* sports bodies in violation of the Olympic principle and resolutions of the United Nations,

Recognizing that participation in sports exchanges with teams selected on the basis of *apartheid* violates the fundamental human rights of the great majority of the people of South Africa and directly abets and encourages the commission of the crime of *apartheid*, as defined in the International Convention on the Suppression and Punishment of the Crime of *Apartheid*, and encourages the racist régime in its pursuit of *apartheid*,

Condemning sports contacts with any country practising *apartheid* and recognizing that participation in *apartheid* in sports condones and strengthens *apartheid* and thereby becomes the legitimate concern of all Governments,

Convinced that an international declaration against *apartheid* in sports would make it possible to take more effective measures at the international and national levels, with a view to completely isolating and eliminating *apartheid*,

Proclaims this International Declaration against *Apartheid* in Sports:

Article 1

States affirm and support this Declaration as an expression of international condemnation of *apartheid* and as a measure to contribute towards the total eradication of the system of *apartheid*, and to this end resolve to take strong action and to exert the greatest possible influence in order to ensure the total elimination of *apartheid* in sports.

Article 2

States shall take all appropriate action to bring about the total cessation of sporting contacts with any country practising *apartheid* and shall refrain from official sponsorship, assistance or encouragement of such contacts.

Article 3

States shall take all appropriate action towards the exclusion or expulsion of any country practising *apartheid* from international and regional sports bodies. They shall give full support to national sports bodies attempting to exclude such countries from membership of international and regional sports associations, or to prevent such countries from participating in sports activities.

Article 4

1. States shall publicly declare and express total opposition to *apartheid* in sports, as well as full and active support for the total boycott of all teams and sportsmen from the racist *apartheid* sports bodies.
2. States shall pursue a vigorous programme of public education aimed at securing strict adherence to the Olympic principle of non-discrimination in sports and widespread national acceptance for the spirit and letter of United Nations resolutions on *apartheid* in sports.
3. Sports bodies shall be actively encouraged to withhold any support from sporting events organized in violation of the Olympic principle and United Nations resolutions. To this end, States shall convey the United Nations resolutions on *apartheid* in sports to all national sports bodies urging them:
    (a) To disseminate such information to all their affiliates and branches;
    (b) To take all necessary action to ensure strict compliance with those
    resolutions.

Article 5

States shall take appropriate actions against their sporting teams and organizations whose members collectively or individually participate in sports activities in any country practising *apartheid* or with teams from a country practising *apartheid*, which in particular shall include:

(a) Refusal to provide financial or other assistance to enable sports bodies, teams or individuals to participate in sports activities in countries practising *apartheid* or with teams and individual sportsmen selected on the basis of *apartheid*;

(b) Refusal to provide financial or other assistance for any purpose to sports bodies whose team members or affiliates participate in such sporting activities;

(c) Withdrawal of access to national sporting facilities to such teams or individuals;

(d) Non-recognition by States of all professional sporting contacts which involve sporting activities in any country practising *apartheid*, or with teams or individual sportsmen selected on the basis of *apartheid*;

(e) Denial and withdrawal of national honours or awards to such teams or individuals;

(f) Denial of official receptions to teams or sportsmen participating in sports activities with teams or individual sportsmen from any country practising *apartheid*.

Article 6

States shall deny visas and/or entry to representatives of sports bodies, members of teams or individual sportsmen from any country practising *apartheid*.

Article 7

States shall establish national regulations and guidelines against participation with *apartheid* in sports and shall ensure that effective means exist for bringing about compliance with such guidelines.

Article 8

States shall co-operate with anti-*apartheid* movements and other organizations which are engaged in promoting the implementation of the principles of this Declaration.

Article 9

States undertake to encourage actively and publicly all official bodies, private enterprises and other groups engaged in promoting, organizing or servicing sports activities to refrain from undertaking any action which in any way supports, assists or enables the organization of activities involving *apartheid* in sports.

Article 10

States shall urge all their regional, provincial and other authorities to take whatever steps are necessary to ensure the strict compliance with the provisions of this Declaration.

Article 11

States agree to use their best endeavours to terminate the practice of *apartheid* in sports in accordance with the principles contained in this Declaration and, to this end, States agree to work towards the prompt preparation and adoption of an international convention on *apartheid* in sports based on the principles contained in this Declaration which would include sanctions for violation of its terms.

Article 12

1. States and international, regional and national sports bodies shall actively support projects, undertaken in collaboration with the Organization of African Unity and the South African liberation movements recognized by it towards the formation of non-racial teams truly representative of South Africa.

2. To this end, States and all appropriate organizations shall encourage, assist and recognize genuine non-racial sports bodies in South Africa endorsed by the Special Committee against *Apartheid*, the Organization of African Unity and the South African liberation movements recognized by it.

3. They shall also give active support to sportsmen and sports administrators

in their opposition to *apartheid* in sports.

Article 13
International, regional and national sports bodies shall uphold the Olympic principle and cease all sports contact with the racist *apartheid* sports bodies.

Article 14
International sporting bodies shall not impose financial or other penalties on affiliated bodies which, in accordance with United Nations resolutions and the spirit of the Olympic Charter, refuse to participate in sports contact with any country practising *apartheid*.

Article 15
National sports bodies shall take appropriate action to persuade their international federation to exclude racist *apartheid* sports bodies from membership and from all international activities.

Article 16
All national Olympic committees shall declare their opposition to *apartheid* in sports, and to sports contact with South Africa, and shall actively encourage all affiliates and constituent members to end all sports contact with South Africa.

Article 17
The provisions of this Declaration concerning the boycott of South African sports teams shall not apply to non-racial sports bodies endorsed by the Special Committee against *Apartheid*, the Organization of African Unity and the South African liberation movements recognized by it and their members.

Article 18
All international, regional, national sports bodies and Olympic committees shall endorse the principles of this Declaration and support and uphold all provisions contained therein.

Document XIII: Text of the Organisation of African Unity's 1981 Resolution on Sporting Links with South Africa

(Resolution 856 (XXXVII), adopted by the OAU Council of Ministers meeting in Nairobi in June 1981)

The Council of Ministers of the Organisation of Africa Unity meeting in its Thirty-seventh Ordinary Session in Nairobi, Kenya, from 15 to 26 June 1981,

Recalling the International Declaration Against Apartheid in Sports adopted by the United Nations General Assembly,

Considering the fact that the racist South African regime is increasingly using sports to break its international isolation,

Aware that the Irish Rugby Football team had recently toured South Africa in violation of the United Nations Resolutions and the International Declaration Against Apartheid in Sports,

Concerned about the fact that South African Springbok Rugby is scheduled to tour New Zealand from July to September 1981,

Recalling all previous resolutions adopted by the OAU in which it appealed to all States, particularly New Zealand, to sever sports links with South Africa,

Recognising that it is within the competence of the New Zealand Government to stop the South African Springbok tour of New Zealand,

Appreciating the initiative of the United Nations Special Committee Against Apartheid to compile a register of sportsmen who participate in sports with apartheid South Africa;

1. CONDEMNS the Irish Rugby Football Union and the New Zealand Rugby Football Union for their violation of the International Declaration Against Apartheid in Sports and other relevant resolutions of the United Nations General Assembly and URGES the Irish Government to take measures which will ensure that no team going to South Africa defy its authority;

2. CALLS UPON the New Zealand Government to take whatever steps are necessary to ensure the cancellation of the Rugby tour;

3. CALLS UPON all Member States to demand the exclusion of New Zealand nationals from all international sporting events if the Springbok rugby tour is allowed to proceed;

4. CALLS UPON Member States to take all necessary measures to ensure that their nationals refrain from participation in all sporting events which include New Zealand nationals;

5. CALLS UPON Member States which are also members of the Commonwealth to request for the cancellation or for the change of the venue and to canvass so that other Members of the Commonwealth in Asia and the Caribbean to request for the same for the forthcoming Commonwealth Finance Ministers' meeting now scheduled to be held in New Zealand later this year if the Springbok Rugby tour to New Zealand is not cancelled;

6. CALLS UPON the African Commonwealth nations to direct (and to canvass so that other Commonwealth nations in Asia and the Caribbean do likewise) their National Olympic Committees/Associations to exert pressure on the appropriate authorities for the exclusion of New Zealand from the Commonwealth Games to be held in Brisbane, Australia in 1982;

7. REQUESTS the Supreme Council for Sport in Africa to keep the OAU Secretary-General informed of the attitude of New Zealand regarding the proposed tour of New Zealand by the Springbok Rugby team and its general policy of allowing its nationals to have sporting links with South Africa in defiance of the International Declaration Against Apartheid in Sport;

8. CALLS UPON governments to ban from entering into their countries, national teams and individuals, to refuse to engage in sporting activities, and to canvass so that Governments of other members of the International Community do the same, with those sportsmen or teams which are listed in the register of the United Nations Special Committee Against Apartheid as having participated in sports with teams in or from racist South Africa.

Document XIV: 'How Muldoon let the Side Down'—Article by the Commonwealth Secretary-General, Sir Shridath Ramphal

Whenever the Commonwealth makes a stand for principle there are usually dissenters who inveigh against it and invoke the spectre of a Commonwealth endangered. South Africa has been at the heart of many of these challenges. Each time, through the courage and vision of its great statesmen—men like Macmillan, Nehru, Pearson, among others—the Commonwealth has stood firm. They had to contend with bigotry and prejudice, with blind resistance to change, sometimes with well-intentioned anxieties about change, and always with much foreboding about the future of the Commonwealth. It was so over the question whether an apartheid South Africa could be welcome to Commonwealth membership, so over the issue of arms sales to South Africa, and so throughout the unhappy Rhodesia chapter. But each time the Commonwealth was right, and was right to have persisted; and each time it grew stronger.

The Springbok tour of New Zealand has faced the Commonwealth with a similar option; to draw back from commitment, or to stand up for its highest principles. Once again, the issue concerns South Africa; for the Gleneagles Agreement is about apartheid. It seeks to eliminate sporting contacts with South Africa. It imposes important obligations on Commonwealth governments and seeks the support of Commonwealth sportsmen in the wider effort to secure for millions in South Africa release from the gross and systematic denial of even their most basic human rights because of their colour. The agreement's premise is that every Commonwealth government is serious in this endeavour.

No amount of innuendo can change the letter or spirit of the Gleneagles Agreement. Its full text was in The Times of July 29. Its language is not ambiguous, nor is its intent; it does not employ 'weasel words' designed to mean all things to all leaders. It is a clear statement of political commitment deeply rooted in principle—that it is 'the urgent duty of each . . . government vigorously to combat the evil of apartheid by withholding any form of support for, and taking every practical step to discourage sporting contacts with South Africa'. No great question of interpretation is at issue.

No one argues, for example, that the Government of New Zealand is obliged by the agreement to use its immigration powers to prohibit sporting contacts. It could use those powers; it has invoked them to discourage other 'cultural exchanges', there is no impediment in law nor, indeed, in the political ethos of the region where other governments have been ready to refuse even transit visas to the South African team.

It has chosen as a matter of policy not to withhold visas—as it always said it would not. But that does not dispose of the government's obligations under Gleneagles. The very act of self-abnegation raises a duty to fulfil them through other means.

Gleneagles left it to each government to find and employ its own means of discouragement; and it held out the assurance of success. Commonwealth leaders were unanimous that in the light of Gleneagles 'there were unlikely to be future sporting contacts of any significance between Commonwealth countries or their nationals and South Africa'. On June 14, 1977 two days after Gleneagles, Mr Muldoon specifically affirmed this: 'We will continue to persuade New Zealand sporting bodies to abandon sporting contacts as we have successfully done for some considerable time now . . . I repeat—I do not think New Zealand will ever play a racially selected South African team again'.

The question is not one of interpretation, it is one of performance; and it is one on which many Commonwealth governments are less than satisfied. And these doubts have grown in recent weeks. The Rugby Union says that the government has never asked it to withdraw the invitation to the Springboks. On July 29 the Acting Prime Minister outlined in Parliament the steps the government had taken in expressing opposition to the tour. He referred to four letters to the Rugby Union expressing 'concern at the invitation', asking the Union 'to reconsider', 'to think again' and 'to weigh the consequences'.

Commonwealth governments could perhaps be forgiven the belief that this was somewhat less than vigorous discouragement of the tour by all practical means. As military forces are now called in to facilitate the tour that belief is bound to sharpen.

In moving their Finance Ministers' meeting from New Zealand—it was scheduled to begin within a few days of the departure of the South African team—Commonwealth governments were simply protecting themselves and the Commonwealth from appearing to condone this ill-conceived tour so alien to the intent of Gleneagles. They were not pronouncing judgment on the question of non-compliance or on New Zealand's record on human rights. It was a necessary reaffirmation of their own commitments to the agreement, and against apartheid.

They, too, have rights; in this matter, they felt a clear duty to exercise them. Their decision was made, of course, in sadness, not retribution, and only after they had failed through every national, regional, Commonwealth and international entreaty to secure the tour's cancellation. For the Rugby Union, in particular, refusal was an act of gross indifference to wider interests: to Commonwealth harmony; to the Commonwealth Games at Brisbane in 1982, and not least, to New Zealand itself.

The Commonwealth, however, cannot be similarly indifferent. It has made its position clear. There will be continuing argument: but it will be on the central issue of where each stands on apartheid and South Africa; for, make no mistake, this is how the issue is seen in the

Commonwealth and in South Africa.

I have no fear for the Commonwealth's future while it remains true to itself. Already, its collective action has helped to undo some of the damage of the Springbok tour. It has made the Commonwealth stronger, not weaker. It will be assailed, of course, by those who prefer to see it less resolute on the question of South Africa. But, as in the past, the Commonwealth will survive these attacks and be the better for the battles it must fight from time to time to maintain its stand for higher principles.

(This article was published in The Times, 5 August 1981).

8. Sponsorship

Sponsorship by South African commerce and industry—including many companies and firms with overseas connections to parents and associates in Europe, America and elsewhere—has always played a major role in the promotion of sport in South Africa. This is one of the aspects of South African sport which helps to illustrate its position within the apartheid system as a whole, and indeed its significance for the regime's continued survival.

The advocates of genuine non-racial sport within South Africa itself have endeavoured to explain, through the assertion that 'there can be no normal sport in an abnormal society', that their campaign has no meaning except in the context of a wider struggle for a free South Africa. The phenomenon of commercial sponsorship—and the parallel links which exist between sport and the apartheid regime's military and defence apparatus—lend convincing weight to their argument.

Sponsorship has in recent years begun to play an extensive role in not only persuading black South Africans to succumb to the government's apartheid sports policy, but also conferring international respectability on the regime by luring top sportsmen and women from overseas to compete in South Africa.

Sport and the apartheid war machine
The sustained militarisation of the apartheid society, furthermore, has led to a situation in which it is no surprise to find that the South African Defence Force (SADF) features prominently in South African sport. Teams drawn from the SADF do well in nearly all sports disciplines and many talented sportsmen are motivated to join the SADF precisely because it provides superior training facilities and ample practice time. A former Springbok rugby captain who served in the army commented, for example, that 'sports facilities in the Defence Force are tremendous'.[1]. The Defence Force is now considering special dispensations for talented sportsmen who need to spend lengthy periods overseas on professional circuits such as tennis and golf.[2].

A similar situation exists in the South African Police (SAP). Charmaine Gale, for example, a Springbok high-jumper, decided at the age of 18 to join the SAP because, as she explained, 'they provide a secure career. I need to train regularly and not all jobs give you the chance to do this'. She said that the police force had in fact contacted her about a possible career while she was still at school.[3].

South Africa's major sports sponsors from commerce and industry are, for their part, members of what was known up to early 1982 as the Defence Advisory Board, a body which advised the Minister of Defence on military matters as they related to the economy. Some of the captains of industry who served on the Defence Advisory Board at the beginning of 1982 included:

Dr. F.J. du Plessis, managing director of SANLAM; Gavin Relly, deputy chairman of Anglo American Corporation; R.J. Goss, managing director of South African Breweries and chairman of the Southern Sun Hotel Group; J.G. van der Horst, chairman of S.A. Mutual Life Assurance Society and Christopher Saunders, chairman of the Tongaat Group (Sugar).[4]

During the first half of 1982 the Defence Advisory Board and related bodies were restructured by the South African government. Representatives of industry and employers' organizations continue to be represented on the Defence Manpower Liaison Committee.[5].

Government funding

Over the financial year 1980-81 the South African government contributed R2,917,000 in administrative grants to the various sports bodies it recognises. Another R151,000 was donated by the government in 1981 to finance visits by overseas sportsmen and women. These participants came mainly from western Europe and the USA.[6]

The South African government is fully aware of the major part to be played by such financial appeasement in diluting international opposition to apartheid sport. The international liaison committee of the officially recognised South African National Olympic Committee is funded entirely by the government through a special annual grant.

Commercial sponsorship

It is a truism to say that the large commercial houses and transnational corporations with interests in South Africa and Namibia have benefited tremendously from apartheid economic policy and will almost certainly continue to reap profits as long as apartheid remains. It can often be to their financial advantage to support apartheid sports bodies and institutions—the basic rationale, indeed, for commercial sponsorship of sporting activity anywhere in the world.

Sponsors and sponsored money play a large part in luring black South African sportsmen and women into joining racial leagues or the government-instigated 'multi-national' competitions. Sponsors 'often assist with the organization, provide attractive prize money and take care of travelling, hotel accommodation expense and provide special equipment, etc.'[7] In recent years, commercial sponsorship has begun to play an important role in providing inflated fees for overseas participants in South African sports competitions.

Big business has been used in an attempt to manipulate black cricket officials. Hassan Howa, former President of the anti-apartheid South African Council on Sport (SACOS) and a veteran fighter against racialism in sport, said that people 'who are compromising in sport all of a sudden take a huge leap in their everyday lives, financially and otherwise. I know of several administrators who were bankrupt at one stage and who are very rich men today. Is this coincidence? I think not'.[8]

On the other hand, anti-apartheid sports bodies are seriously undermined by being deprived of sponsorship. Quite often they are told indirectly that they ought to subscribe to the policy of multi-national sport before their requests are considered.

Dr Errol Vawda, President of the anti-apartheid Natal Council on Sport, explained in April 1982 that 'large national and transnational companies with the establishment have come together in order to control sponsorships. Obviously this sponsorship must be given only to those according to their rules and not the true non-racial sports movement.' He went on to state that 'the massive injection of money into certain sports groups is calculated to weaken the will of the underprivileged'.[9]

Dr Vawda was probably referring to a recently formed organisation, the Association of South African Sponsors. A few weeks later, Hassan Howa told delegates to the 1982 annual meeting of the South African Cricket Board that 'it is unlikely that the South African Cricket Board will get sponsorship this year'.[10] He laid the blame firmly at the door of the Association of South African Sponsors, and said that the Association was deliberately trying to kill the advance of non-racial sport. Hassan Howa went on to say about this new organization:

'Obviously, those who refuse to dance to their tune will get nothing. This is no more than organised blackmail—which has to be stopped'.[11]

During the first half of 1982 alone South African companies spent astronomical amounts to attract overseas golfers, cricketers, tennis players, swimmers and footballers to the country. All the events in which these sportsmen and women participated were a financial flop but nevertheless South Africa tried to gain extraordinary political mileage out of the fact that overseas sports stars competed in South Africa. It is possible that there was secret government involvement in these projects.

South African Breweries (SAB)
The South African Breweries is by far the largest single sponsor of apartheid sport. Together with its subsidiary company, the Southern Sun Hotel Group, SAB bears a major responsibility for luring international sports stars to South Africa.

In February 1982 the South African Breweries spent £1.2 million to persuade a team of English cricketers to play a series of matches in South Africa.[12]

The reported figure of between £40,000 and £50,000 offered to each touring player was far in excess of an equivalent tour in any other part of the world.[13]

In July 1982 a group of footballers, mostly British, defied an official international ban and toured South Africa to earn highly inflated fees. An

English international footballer was offered £250,000 for the six-match tour which was sponsored by the South African Breweries for a reported sum of £1 million.[14].

Besides its efforts internationally South African Breweries spends over R1 million annually on sports sponsorship at national level. The major benefactors are rugby (R250,000), football (R250,000) and cricket (R70,000) (figures for 1980).[15]

The Southern Sun Hotel Group, similarly, spends millions of rands each year to lure international sports stars, entertainers and artists to South Africa. As the owner, manager and developer of a chain of hotels and other enterprises in South Africa's bantustans, including Sun City in Bophuthatswana, it has played a key role in conferring respectability on the 'homeland' concept. In 1979 and 1980, for example, Southern Sun spent millions of rands in arranging World Heavyweight Boxing Championship bouts, the second in Bophuthatswana. According to the company itself, these gave the Group 'huge exposure internationally through the TV networks and the press media'.[16]

In late 1980 Southern Sun tried to persuade two top international tennis stars, John McEnroe and Bjorn Borg, to play a challenge match in Bophuthatswana. The two superstars were to share a R900,000 fee with an extra R120,000 for the winner of the match which was to be televised worldwide.[17] This match was aborted because McEnroe refused to provide apartheid with international respectability.

Southern Sun has long been suspected of receiving government funds. In January 1982 doubts were again raised as to how the Group obtained over R1.25 million to finance international golf's biggest prize-money for a tournament in South Africa—held in Bophuthatswana in December 1981. The opposition Progressive Reform Party said it would raise the issue in parliament to challenge the South African government to prove that it did not help finance the project.[18] As usual the government denied the charge.

Other companies involved
The following are some of the other important companies known to have sponsored sports events and activities in South Africa:

Adidas
Gave an undisclosed sum in 1980 for Junior Tennis.[19]

Altech Electronics
Promised R300,000 to the 1982 South African Open Tennis Championships.[20]

Barclays Bank
Regular sponsorship of cricket coaching, in the region of R35,000 annually; provides money for various other coaching projects.[21]

Benson & Hedges
Sponsored a national interprovincial cricket competition due to extend over three years (1981-84). The total sum promised was reported in 1981 to be R2 million.[22]

Blue Circle Products
Regular sponsorship of athletics (R35,000 - 1980 figure).[23]

British Petroleum (BP)
Regular sponsorship of soccer (R40,000 - 1981 figure).[24]

Casio Products
Sponsors football (amount undisclosed).[25]

Checkers
Gave R35,000 for cricket coaching in 1980.[26]

Coca Cola
Gave R5,000 to the Black Tennis Foundation in 1978.[27]

Colgate Palmolive
Sponsors golf, athletics and tennis. Colgate has an annual budget of about R120,000 (1978-79 figures) for the promotion of multi-national sport.[28]

Datsun Nissan
Regular sponsorship of the Football Professional Soccer League. The figure for 1982 was R65,000.[29]
  Regular sponsorship of cricket (R125,000 in 1980) and golf (R75,000 in 1978).[30]

General Motors
Began in 1981 to sponsor surf life saving on a regular basis (figure undisclosed).[31]

Holiday Inn
Regular sponsorship of various coaching clinics (figures undisclosed).[32]
  Annual sponsorship of football (figure undisclosed)[33], athletics (R70,000). horse racing (R120,000) and golf (R35,000) (all figures for 1978-79).[34]

IGI Insurance
Has provided a tennis coaching clinic for blacks only. The sum involved (1981) was R20,000.[35]

International Harvester
Gave R5,000 for a cricket coaching project in the Transvaal in 1980.[36]

Isotonic Games
Regular sponsorship of women's squash (amount undisclosed).[37]

Kronenbrau
Regular sponsorship of cricket coaching. The figure for 1980 was R40,000.[38]

Mainstay
Regular sponsorship of soccer (R85,000 - 1980 figure).[39]

Mobil Oil
Regular sponsorship of various coaching projects. The figure for 1982 was R25,000.[40]

Nashua
Has sponsored the South African Grand Prix on a regular basis. In 1980 the sum involved was reported to be R100,000.[41]

Pro Nutro
Regular sponsorship of the annual Sporting Greats Competition (figure undisclosed).[42]

Sales House
Regular sponsorship of soccer (R25,000 - 1981 figure).[43]

Sigma
Sponsored the South African Defence Force (SADF) boxing tour to Chile and Paraguay in 1982 (figure undisclosed).[44] Also sponsors golf (R130,000 - 1980 figure)[45] and tennis (R65,000 1978-79 figure).[46]

South African Dairy Board
Regular sponsorship of rugby (R65,000 - 1980 figure, R35,000 - 1981 figure).[47]

South African Sugar Association
Sponsors the international provinicial tennis circuit which attracts several overseas players. (Total sponsorship figures not disclosed).

Standard Bank
Regular sponsorship of the Tennis International Match, held annually in South Africa, usually against a US team (figure undisclosed).[48]

Stellenbosch Farmers Winery
Sponsored the 1982 South African Athletics tour to Europe (figure undisclosed),[49] regular sponsorship of athletics (R125,000 in 1980).[50]

9. The United Nations Register of Sports Contacts with South Africa

On 24 October 1980, the United Nations Special Committee against Apartheid announced that it would soon draw up a list of sportsmen/women and administrators who violated the sports ban on South Africa. The United Nations Press Release of 24 October 1980 stated:

'The international community cannot but take appropriate action to stop sports events of this kind in South Africa. In this connection the Director of the Centre against Apartheid, Mr E.S. Reddy, announced today that in accordance with decisions by the Special Committee, the Centre has initiated the compilation of a register of sportsmen, sports administrators and others who flagrantly violated the sports boycott against South Africa. The register will be made available to governments and organizations all over the world to facilitate action against the collaborators with the apartheid regime.'[1]

Immediately thereafter the South African Non-Racial Olympic Committee (SAN-ROC) released an unofficial advance list of sportsmen and sportswomen who competed in sports events in South Africa.

Kenya and Nigeria banned several British tennis players whose names appeared on the SAN-ROC list from participating in tournaments in their respective countries. In May 1981, the United Nations Special Committee Against Apartheid published its first *Register of Sports Contacts with South Africa.*

The action of Kenya and Nigeria in banning the British tennis players was followed by the expelling of Robin Jackman, an English cricketer, from Guyana for his association with apartheid sport.

The press, most British sports officials and apparently the British government were thrown into confusion when these sportsmen and women were made unwelcome by some countries which strongly opposed sports links with South Africa.

A great deal of heat was generated by the so-called 'blacklist'. Wild allegations were made about the unfairness and there were even anti-libertarian implications drawn from compiling such a Register or taking action against individual sportsmen and women for their 'private' decision to play in South Africa.

Reasons for Register
In all the major team sports—with the exception of rugby—South Africa has

been isolated relatively successfully. South Africa has been expelled or suspended from international participation in almost all disciplines and many governments have discouraged sports exchanges with South Africa.

Although most international sports federations have prevented South Africa from participating in world championships, South Africa, nevertheless, is still allowed to invite teams and individuals in some disciplines to its country by virtue of the fact that its international affiliations in these disciplines have not been cancelled—because of the goodwill of western countries.

Western countries, either because of their overwhelming majority in numbers or because of voting systems which result in their having the majority of votes, have always protected South Africa from total expulsion in several sports disciplines. Motions to exclude South Africa from sports disciplines such as tennis, golf, gymnastics, fencing, archery, shooting, yacht racing, equestrian sport, etc. failed not because racial discrimination in South African sport was not proved, but because of western sympathies for white South Africa.

The Supreme Council for Sport in Africa and SAN-ROC, greatly frustrated by the active sabotage by western countries of the international sports boycott campaign, enthusiastically welcomed the United Nations Register. The Register would now enable countries to identify culprits and to initiate sanctions against them for blatantly violating the sports ban on South Africa.

The United Nations Register was only intended, and is in practice used, for strengthening the international sports boycott on South Africa. Individuals and teams participating in football, athletics, swimming, weightlifting, etc. are barred from competing in South Africa by their respective federations. This is because these federations have expelled South Africa and will not condone exchanges with South Africa. The Register now offers sportsmen and women of international sports federations which protect South Africa's membership by virtue of the fact that western countries hold the majority of votes, this very same choice.

Countries which are strongly anti-apartheid feel 'let-down' by those sportsmen and women who, by their competing in South Africa, are providing a boost for apartheid sport and are delaying its ultimate demise. Many African and Caribbean governments have now announced that they will bar sportsmen and women who compete in South Africa from their respective countries.

Effects of the Register on apartheid sport
South Africa's response to the UN initiative has taken the form of providing even larger prize money for its own professional tournaments in tennis and golf or by paying astronomical appearance fees for members of team sports such as cricket and football.

The publication of the Register nevertheless forced many prospective sports visitors to South Africa to reconsider their position. Several sportsmen and women began to examine their consciences. Some realised, for the first time, that they were being used by South Africa to advertise apartheid politics internationally. Several others opted out of South African competitions fearing that lucrative opportunities and sports grounds in other parts of the world might soon be closed to them if they continued to compete in South Africa. But others refused to relinquish their ties with South African sport. The latter were by and large either mediocre players or players reaching the end of their careers who had little to lose.

Overall fewer people competed in South Africa in comparable tournaments in 1982 than during 1981. For instance the South African Tennis Grand Prix which normally attracts between 40 and 50 overseas stars attracted only eleven in 1982.

Conclusion

During the first half of 1982 alone more than $5 million was spent by South Africa on inviting teams of golfers, cricketers and footballers to visit the country to boost apartheid. Many individual swimmers, cricketers, waterskiers, surfers, iceskaters, rugby, tennis and squash players were also invited to South Africa with all their expenses paid.

Rugby administrators who were invited not only had all their expenses paid but the wives of some of them were even presented with expensive necklaces. The President of the South African Rugby Board, Dr. Danie Craven, referring to presents handed over to New Zealand rugby officials said:

> 'If we could buy goodwill through the gifts we gave to the New Zealand rugby councillors and their wives I would suggest that we start a campaign to buy the goodwill of all the demonstrators.'[1]

Craven's remark, while possibly intended in a spirit of bravado, nevertheless exposed deep-rooted anxieties shared by the regime and its supporters at the growing success of the international sports boycott of apartheid. While the non-co-operation of certain sports bodies in the west has undoubtedly undermined the effectiveness of the campaign to isolate apartheid, it has, overall, made important and sustained advances.

The success of the international sports boycott and the knowledge that thousands and indeed millions of people around the world support their cause, have greatly boosted the morale of South Africa's black sportsmen and women and sports adminstrators. Together with sports fans and ordinary people throughout South Africa, they have stepped up their resistance to government sports policies. There is no doubt that the coming months and years will see a further acceleration of activity against apartheid sport, both inside South Africa and internationally, and that this will continue to make its contribution to the ultimate destruction of apartheid itself.

Is the world playing games with South Africa?

While the dispute rages over the Moscow Olympics, no one suggests that Soviet athletes should be penalised. They have competed freely (and rightly) at the Winter Olympics, and will not be cold-shouldered at future meetings elsewhere.

However, with South Africa it is the athletes themselves who are denied by the International Olympic Committee's boycott the ultimate goal of competing internationally.

Why?

Because it is alleged that South African racial policies deny equal opportunities to black athletes.

Today, this is, quite simply, untrue. The controlling bodies of sport in South Africa are autonomous.

Their constitutions are non-racial, and no barriers of a racial or other nature are imposed by the government. No laws deny the black player the opportunities of the white.

The sceptic may say: so what? The plain answer is that in nine months of 1978, 2,615 mixed sporting events took place, including 44 at international level. Since then, mixed sport has become so commonplace that statistics do not merit keeping.

South African athletes are being ostracised for political reasons, while the sportsmen of many other nations whose regimes and policies could be open to censure are free to compete internationally.

Is this playing the game?

Issued by the Information Service, South African Embassy, London.

Advertisement placed in the British press by the South African Embassy in London, February 1980.

Advertisement placed in the South African press by South African Breweries for the rebel cricket tour of South Africa in March 1982.

Lion Lager presents

THE SAB INTERNATIONALS

Seventeen of the finest players in the world, some of them straight from the World Cup. Included are players from England, Belgium, Yugoslavia, Argentina, Scotland.

These are the SAB Internationals, brought to you by Lion Lager. They're probably the strongest team ever assembled. And they're here in South Africa to give you the soccer excitement of your life!

Don't miss your chance to see the SAB Internationals in action against the best that Chiefs, Swallows, Pirates, Hellenic and the rest can throw at them.

It's the World Cup soccer you never saw. Brought to you by Lion Lager.

Friday 16 July	Greenpoint 8.00 pm. SAB Internationals vs Hellenic/Spurs/United.
Sunday 18 July	Orlando Stadium 3.00 pm. SAB Internationals vs Orlando Pirates.
Wednesday 21 July	Ellis Park 7.30 pm. SAB Internationals vs Highlands/Swallows/Dynamos/Wits.
Sunday 25 July	Kings Park Rugby Stadium Durban 3.00 pm. SAB Internationals vs Durban City Invitation Team.
Wednesday 28 July	Harry Oppenheimer Stadium Vaal Reefs 7.30 pm. SAB Internationals vs Kaiser's XI
Friday 30 July	Ellis Park 7.30 pm. SAB Internationals vs Kaiser Chiefs.

Unhurried lagering unzips more taste.

Advertisement placed in the South African Press by South African Breweries for the rebel soccer tour of South Africa in July 1982.

The Springboks of tomorrow need a little help from their friends.

Friends like Mobil, who for many years have invested big money and hundreds of thousands of coaching hours in the future of South African sport.

Friends like Garth le Roux, Omar Henry and Peter Kirsten, who, as Mobil coaches, are giving their talent and time to encourage young cricketers of all races.

Mobil provides friends in other sports too. Big names in soccer, like Kevin Keegan and Eusebio who have been brought out to this country to help train our future Peles.

And Springboks like Leon Norgarb to coach our future tennis stars.

South Africa's youth share the same dreams and ambitions of youth all around the world — to wear the national colours, for us the green and gold.

Mobil and its people are committed to improving the quality of life for all South Africans, and especially to the development of young, untried sports talent for the future.

Mobil

With us you are Number One.

Advertisement placed in the South African press by Mobil Oil, March 1982.

A cartoon in the *Rand Daily Mail,* **January 1982.**

This meeting at the University of Natal, called by students to protest against the rebel English Cricket tour of South Africa in March 1982, was later disrupted by pro-government white students.

Appendix I: South Africa's Present Position in International Sport

Third World and Socialist countries have campaigned for the last 20 years for the total isolation of South African sport. Initially the powerful western bloc of countries vetoed the expulsion of South Africa from many international sports federations.

Since 1966 the Supreme Council for Sport in Africa (SCSA) has co-ordinated efforts to ban South Africa from international sport. With the assistance of several sympathetic governments South Africa has been barred from nearly all the major international sports events. Nevertheless, western countries still manage to protect South Africa's membership of many international sports federations.

Summary:

A. Olympic Sports	International federation or association	South Africa's status
Olympic Games	International Olympic Committee (IOC)	suspended from participating in the 1964 Games but the suspension was lifted in 1968. Intervention by African countries forced the IOC to re-impose the suspension. Expelled in May 1970.
Archery	Federation Internationale de Tir a l'Arc (FITA)	full member but only allowed participation at discretion of host country.
Athletics	International Amateur Athletic Federation (IAAF)	SA expelled from IAAF on 22 July 1976 at its Montreal congress. (Veterans athletics—see Other Sports)
Basketball	Federation Internationale de Basketball Amateur (FIBA)	expelled in 1978
Bobsleigh & tobogganing	Federation Internationale de Bobsleigh et de Tobogganing (FIBT)	not a member, this sport is not practised in South Africa.
Boxing—amateur	Association Internationale de Boxe Amateur (AIBA)	expelled in 1968. (Professional Boxing—see Other Sports)
Canoeing	Federation Internationale de Canoe (FIC)	conditionally suspended by FIC. South Africans allowed to participate as individuals in certain competitions.
Cycling	Federation Internationale Amateur de Cyclisme (FIAC)	application for membership of FIAC by SA Cycling Federation rejected in 1970; decision confirmed in 1973.

88

Equestrian sport	Federation Equestre Internationale (FEI)	full member
Fencing	Federation Internationale d'Escrime (FIE)	full member, but not allowed to compete in world championships. However SA arranges bilateral matches with some West European countries.
Football	Federation Internationale de Football Association (FIFA)	expelled in July 1976
Gymnastics	Federation Internationale de Gymnastique (FIG)	full member but forced out of world championships by East European countries. International participation restricted to competitions in USA, Switzerland and Israel.
Handball	International Handball Federation (IHF)	SA's application for membership rejected by the IHF Congress in London, August 1982.
Hockey	Federation Internationale de Hockey (FIH)	full member of FIH but excluded from world championships through pressure from African members.
Ice Hockey	International Ice Hockey Federation (IIHF)	full member but international participation restricted to inviting teams and individuals to SA.
Judo	International Judo Federation (IJF)	SA has declined to submit formal application for membership in view of its certain rejection.
Luge	Federation Internationale de Luge de Course (FIL)	has not applied to join. No association in SA.
Pentathlon & Biathlon	Union Internationale de Pentathlon Moderne et Biathlon (UIPMB)	full member, but does not take part in international biathlon events.
Rowing	Federation Internationale des Societes d'Aviron (FISA)	full member, but has been barred from participating in world championships. International participation restricted to Henley Regatta (England) and inviting competitors to SA.

A. Olympic Sports	International federation or association	South Africa's status
Shooting	Union Internationale de Tir (UIT)	full member but may only participate as individuals by invitation of host country. In small-bore rifle shooting South Africa is not allowed to take part in world championships but invites a few international competitors to its shooting events.
Skating	International Skating Union (ISU)	full member but not allowed to compete in world championships
Skiing (snow)	Federation Internationale de Ski (FIS)	full member but barred from international competition.
Swimming	Federation Internationale de Natation Amateur (FINA)	expelled in 1973
Volleyball	Federation Internationale de Volley-Ball (FIVB)	has not applied for membership as SA is aware that it will be rejected.
Weightlifting	International Weightlifting Federation (IWF)	expelled in 1972; has established bilateral exchanges with Taiwan, another expelled member.
Wrestling	Federation Internationale de Lutte Amateur (FILA)	expelled in 1970
Yacht racing	International Yacht Racing Union (IYRU)	full member but only takes part in some divisions by invitation of host country.

B. Other Sports	International federation or association	South Africa's status
Aerobatics	No recognised federation	takes part in activities loosely assembled by European and American countries.
Angling	Confederation Mondiale de la Peche Sportive	membership suspended; there are various other angling and fishing organizations which allow SA to participate
Badminton	International Badminton Federation	retains membership but has been barred from participation in world championships
Baseball	International Association of Amateur Baseball	suspended from all international activity

Bodybuilding	International Bodybuilding Federation (IBBF)	full member but has been barred from participation in world championships
Boxing (Professional)	World Boxing Council (WBC) World Boxing Assoc (WBA)	SA is a member of WBA only. WBA Executive is heavily loaded with white South Africans and consequently dominates its administration.
Bowls	International Bowls Association	full member but barred from taking part in world championships. SA's international competition restricted, by and large, to bilateral links with the UK.
Casting	International Casting Federation	member but only participates by invitation of host country
Chess	International Chess Federation	expelled in 1978
Cricket—men's	International Cricket Conference (ICC, formerly Imperial Cricket Conference)	SA Cricket Association ceased to be a member of the ICC in 1961, after SA left the Commonwealth, but it retained bilateral relations with ICC member countries until 1970
Cricket—women's	International Women's Cricket Association	full member. Not allowed to participate in world championships
Cycling	Union Cycliste Internationale (UCI)	although SA is not a member of UCI some UCI members participate in SA. UCI not recognised by IOC.
Darts	World Darts Federation (WDF)	the WDF, inaugurated in London on 21 March 1976, has accepted the anti-apartheid SA Darts Board of Control (SADBOC) as a member. SADBOC has pledged not to accept any invitation to play in world fixtures until there is complete freedom in the movement of play in SA.
Golf	International Golf Association	full member but particpates in world championships by negotiation with host country (both amateur and professional). Individuals barred from nearly all Third World countries.

B. Other Sports	International federation or association	South Africa's status
Karate	World Union of Karatedo Organisations	full member but participates by invitation of host country
Motorcycling	Federation Internationale Motocyliste	full member and participates in championships in most countries
Motor cars	World Grand Prix Motor Championship	SA Grand Prix forms part of the circuit (international Grand Prix racing is sponsored mainly by commercial concerns dealing with motor parts and accessories)
Netball	International Federation of Netball Associations	expelled in 1979
Orienteering	International Orienteering Federation	Not a member
Disabled sport	International Sports Organisation for the Disabled	full member and allowed to participate in most activities as nearly all activities held in England
Power Boats	Union Internationale Motonautique	full member and participates in all activities as member. Is composed exclusively of western countries.
Power Lifting	International Power Lifting Federation	application rejected in 1979
Roller-skating	Federation Internationale de Roller-Skating	full member but barred from world championships
Rugby	Federation Internationale de Rugby Amateur (FIRA); International Rugby Board (IRB)	not a member of FIRA; full member of IRB, along with England, Scotland, Wales, Ireland, New Zealand, Australia and France. IRB member countries arrange bilateral tours
Silent sports	International Committee of Silent Sport	full member but not allowed to participate in any activity
Softball	International Softball Federation	full member but is only allowed to participate in competitions by negotiation with host country

Squash	International Squash Association	Participation in world championships subject to negotiation with the host country
Table Tennis	International Table Tennis Federation (ITTF)	white SA Table Tennis Union expelled from ITTF in 1956 and anti-apartheid SA Table Tennis Board (SATTB) accepted as a member. After 1957, when SATTB members returning from participating in the World Championships had their passports confiscated, the SATTB announced that it would not participate in international competitions until conditions in SA were conducive to non-racial play at all levels. The SA government has never accepted the SATTB and lists SA as expelled from international table tennis.
Taekwondo	World Taekwondo Federation	has not applied for membership knowing that it will be rejected
Tenpin Bowling	Federation Internationale des Quilleurs	not a member
Tennis	International Tennis Federation (ITF)	full member but barred from Davis Cup competition by decision of ITF management committee on 23 March 1970; excluded again in 1972 but since 1973 has been allowed to play in various American zones. Excluded from both Davis Cup and Federation Cup competitions since February 1978, when an ITF Commission visited SA to investigate tennis administration. Individuals barred from many countries.
Trampolining	Internationaler Trampolin-Verband	full member and enjoys international participation because most members are from western countries
Tug-of-War	Tug-of-War International Federation	full member but takes part in international competitions by negotiation with host country

B. Other Sports	International federation or association	South Africa's status
Underwater sport	Confederation Mondiale des Activities Subaquatiques	full member but only participates in competitions by invitation of host country
University sports	Federation Internationale de Sport Universitaire	not a member but has bilateral relations with some West European countries
Veterans' Athletics	World Association of Veterans' Athletics	full member and participates in most competitions
Water-skiing	Union Mondiale de Ski Nautique	full member but excluded from world championships. Takes part in international water-skiing events staged in Italy, France and West Germany by invitation

South Africa boasts membership of several other federations not listed above. However these tend to be sports in which the participants are drawn from only a minority of countries:

billiards and snooker
croquet
cruising
curling
game-fishing
jukskei
model power boating
model yachting
pony sport
surf life saving
surf riding
target casting
veteran and vintage cars[1]

The Minister of Sport and Recreation said in Parliament on 25 March 1980 that South Africa enjoyed full international participation in target casting, light tackle boat angling, game fishing angling, rock and surf angling and skiboat angling. Other sports mentioned by the Minister in this context included hang gliding, parachuting, power flying and hot air ballooning.[2] On 26 February 1981, the Minister of Sport and Recreation said that South Africa had been re-admitted to the European Fishing Sports Administration (game fishing) and the International Anglers' Federation (freshwater angling).[3]

Appendix II: Sports Administration in South Africa

In some sports in South Africa umbrella bodies have been created to give the impression that these disciplines have single controlling bodies. However, it is in such bodies that segregation is most glaring. In other sports some black clubs and/or regional units have been given selective affiliation to white controlling bodies. By selective affiliation it is meant that only certain privileges and provisions are open to black members and it does not imply that all facilities are thrown open to the black members.

The following is a summary of the administration and activity of the various sports disciplines in South Africa:

ORGANISATIONS WHICH WORK WITHIN THE FRAMEWORK OF GOVERNMENT POLICY AND ARE THEREFORE OFFICIALLY RECOGNISED

ANTI-APARTHEID ORGANISATIONS WHICH REFUSE TO COLLABORATE WITH THE GOVERNMENT

National

South African Olympic and National Games Association. White controlled with token black representation

South African Council on Sport. Enjoys observer status with the Supreme Council for Sport in Africa

South African Sports Federation Exclusively white

Athletics

* **South African Amateur Athletic Union.** White controlled. Black membership almost totally from mining areas where mining authorities provide facilities for African migrant male employees. The (African) **South African Amateur Athletic Federation** which administers, through white officials, athletics for the Africans, is now reported to be dormant.

South African Amateur Athletics Board. Has affiliates in the provinces of Natal, Transvaal and Western Province (Cape)

Archery

* **South African National Archery Association.** Exclusively white with the exception of a Coloured paraplegic club (Protea Club of Cape Town) which has been incorporated into a white club for membership purposes. This was done through the instigation of the SA Sports Assoc for the Physically Disabled.

None

95

Badminton

* **South African Badminton Union.**
The Union reported to the British
Sports Council in 1980 that 'non-
white' participation was
approximately 7 per cent.

Western Province Badminton Union.
(Cape Province)

Baseball

* **South African Baseball
Federation.** White

There are several Coloured
organizations in the Cape Province.

Boxing

Amateur
The **South African National Boxing
Federation** is the administrative
umbrella body consisting of:
   **South African Amateur Boxing
   Association.** (White)
   **South African Amateur Boxing
   Board.** (Coloured)
   **South African Amateur Boxing
   Union.** (African)
Professional
South African Boxing Board of Control.
This Board administers overall control
of professional boxing. The Board
members are appointed by the
Government.

None

**South African Professional
Boxing Unity**

Cricket

South African Cricket Union.
(approx. 16,500 players)

South African Cricket Board.
(approx. 5,000 players)

Cycling

* **South African Cycling Federation.**
(approx. 1,000 cyclists)

South African Cycling Board.
(approx. 100 cyclists)

Darts

* **South African Darts Association.**

South African Darts Board of Control.
This Board is affiliated to the World
Darts Federation but does not
participate in international
competitions in accordance with
resolutions of the United Nations,
Organisation of African Unity and
Supreme Council for Sport in Africa.
(See Appendix I)

96

Sports for the Disabled

* **South African Sports Association for Paraplegics and other Physically Disabled.** This association caters largely for whites, but recently blacks have been allowed to participate in provincial and national competitions and some blacks are included in its touring sides to give respectability to apartheid.

None

Fencing

* **South African Fencing Association.** It is believed that a Coloured club from the Cape Town area is affiliated to this association.

None

Football (Soccer)

Football Council of South Africa. Umbrella body existing in name only but supposedly consisting of:

    Football Association of South Africa. A white body which administers a professional league known as the National Football League

    South African National Football Association. An African body which administers a professional league known as the National Professional Soccer League

    South African Football Association. (Coloured)

South African Soccer Federation. Initially the Soccer Federation controlled all black football in South Africa but government and police intimidation forced most Africans to play their football in the so-called townships. Township football is controlled by government administration boards.

    The South African Soccer Federation administers a professional leagueknown as the Football Professional League.

Golf

* **South African Golf Union.** Club membership is strictly white but recently a few Coloured and Asian members have been admitted into a few clubs on a selective basis.

    There are two professional golf associations—one for whites and the other for blacks.

Durban Golf Club.

Gymnastics

* **South African Amateur Gymnastic
Union.** This union has an African
body (the **Soweto Amateur Gymnastic
Union**) and a Coloured body (the
**Western Province Gymnastic
Association**) affiliated to it.

None

Hockey

* **South African Men's Hockey
Association**
**South African Women's
Hockey Association**
The Women's Association has a few
Coloured Clubs.

**South African Hockey Board
(Men)
South African Women's Hockey
Board**

Judo

* **South African Judo Union** There are
some black clubs in townships such as
Soweto

Some loosely organized clubs

Karate

* **National Amateur Karate
Association of South Africa**
Has a few African and Coloured clubs.

Several provincial associations

Lifesaving

* **Surf Lifesaving Association of
South Africa** Has a few black clubs
affiliated to it but only allowed to take
part in authorised competitions
* **South African Lifesaving Association**
An offshoot of the Royal Lifesaving
Society (London), it merely conducts
tests and examinations in still water.

None

Netball

* **South African Women's Netball
Association** Has affiliated to it the
**African Women's Netball Association of
South Africa** (membership only in
Soweto)

South African Netball Union

Rugby

South African Rugby Board (White)
South African Rugby Football Federation (SARFF) (Coloured)
South African Rugby Association (SARA) (African)
SARFF and SARA enjoy subservient affiliation to the white board and these two black bodies are allowed to field one team each in the white 2nd division inter-provincial league

South African Rugby Union

Softball

* **South African Softball Association**

Loosely organized national body

Squash

* **South African Squash Rackets Association** Has affiliated to it a few Indian clubs from Natal but it has been reported that many are joining the anti-apartheid unit.

Several provincial units with strongest support in Natal.

Swimming

* **South African Amateur Swimming Union** (exclusively white)

Amateur Swimming Association of South Africa

Table Tennis

* **South African Table Tennis Union**

South African Table Tennis Board
Gained affiliation to the International Table Tennis Federation when the White Union was expelled.
   The Board participated in the 1957 World Championships in Sweden but on its return team members had their passports confiscated by the government. Thereafter Board members were not allowed to leave the country to participate in international competitions. Does not now participate in international competitions in accordance with United Nations and other resolutions.

Tennis

* **South African Tennis Union**
  Has a few individual black members

Tennis Association of South Africa

Volleyball

* **South African Volleyball Association**
  (exclusively white)

Several provincial associations

Weightlifting and Bodybuilding

* **South African Amateur Bodybuilding Union**
* **South African Amateur Weightlifting Union**

South African Amateur Weightlifting and Bodybuilding Federation

As nearly all the other sports practised in South Africa are of a technical nature, i.e. they require specialised equipment and facilities and are therefore very expensive) participation, control and administration are exclusively white. Although their administration is strictly racial and blacks are barred from participation by virtue of closed club membership, many of them nevertheless still enjoy international affiliation.

* Recognised by the South African Government as white organizations catering for the white population group of South Africa.[1]

Appendix III: Government Figures for Sports Participation

During 1980, the South African government released the following figures for the numbers of persons, excluding school children, who 'actively participated' in various kinds of sport:

Sport	Whites (a)	Africans (b)	Coloureds (c)	Indians (d)
Aerobatics	40	—	—	
Aircraft, Home Built	4,500	—	—	
Angling, Freshwater	11,392	—	551	
Angling, Game Fish	1,300	—	—	
Angling, Light Tackle Boat	3,345	—	—	
Angling, Rock and Surf	7,000	—	—	
Angling, Skiboat	5,281	—	—	
Athletics	16,000	1,861	1,189	
Athletics, Masters	5,000	—	—	
Archery	500	—	—	
Badminton	11,000	78	32	
Baseball	4,800	—	506	
Basketball	4,800	1,300	—	
Billiards and Snooker	2,500	—	—	
Blind Bowlers	350	—	—	
Boat, Model Power	200	—	—	

Sport	Whites (a)	Africans (b)	Coloureds (c)	Indians (d)
Boat, Power	1,000	—	—	
Boat, Scale Model	110	—	—	
Ballooning, Hot Air	25	—	—	
Body Building	5,000	—	239	
Bowling, Tenpin	5,000	—	—	
Bowls (men)	39,346	220	170	
Bowls (women)	28,606	—	—	
Boxing	2,670	8,620	1,635	
Canoeing	1,700	—	413	
Casting, Target	286	—	—	
Chess	15,000	—	—	
Cricket (men)	41,000	2,939	4,380	
Cricket (women)	200	—	—	
Croquet	200	—	—	
Cruising	1,081	—	—	
Cycling	973	50	254	
Darts (men)	2,500	—	—	
Darts (women)	422	—	—	
Equestrian	4,800	—	90(e)	
Fencing	500	—	44	
Football (Soccer)	400,000	128,222	23,061	
Formula 'K'	250	—	—	
Flying, Power	4,371	—	—	
Gliding	600	—	—	
Golf (men)	41,000	4,527	201	
Golf (women)	8,000	—	—	
Gymnastics	6,000	78	4,000	
Handball	150	—	—	
Hang Gliding	400	—	—	
Hockey (men)	8,000	—	2,610	
Hockey (women)	7,680	—	—	
Hockey, Ice	250	—	—	
Hockey, Roller-Skating	340	—	—	
Judo	15,000	841	1,424	
Jukskei	12,000	—	—	
Karate	11,500	5,582	253	
Korfball	16,000	—	—	
Life Saving	1,961	—	77	
Life Saving, Surf	2,493	—	—	
Model Radio Drivers	200	—	—	
Motor Sport	10,000	—	—	
Netball	40,000	9,638	6,367	
Parachuting	750	—	—	
Paraplegic Sport	2,427	—	47	
Pentathlon	2,000	—	—	
Polo	400	—	—	
Polocrosse	516	—	—	
Pony Club	3,000	—	—	
Radio Flyers	1,050	—	—	
Roller-Skating	248	—	—	
Rowing	1,650	—	—	
Rifle, National	1,100	—	—	

Sport	Whites (a)	Africans (b)	Coloureds (c)	Indians (d)
Rugby	189,146	17,025	19,284	
Schwinger	100	—	—	
Skating, Ice	2,875	—	—	
Shooting, Target	—	—	480	
Shooting, Air Rifle	150	—	—	
Shooting, Clay Pigeon	1,954	—	—	
Shooting, Pistol	4,000	—	—	
Shooting, Practical	2,000	—	—	
Shooting, Service	1,000	—	—	
Shooting, Small Bore	550	—	—	
Snow Skiing	1,342	—	—	
Softball	3,000	2,485	871	
Squash (men)	25,000	—	—	
Squash (women)	4,000	—	—	
Surfing, Paddle	340	—	—	
Surf-riding	2,475	—	39	
Swimming	10,000	2,138	1,073	
Table Tennis	2,800	2,520	777	
Tennis	85,000	10,498	3,860	
Tennisquoits	1,500	265	—	
Tug-of-War	1,600	—	—	
Underwater Sport	3,000	—	—	
Veteran Motor Sport	183	—	—	
Volleyball	2,000	132	—	
Walking	—	—	17	
Weightlifting	657	1,604(f)	408	
Wrestling	7,300	70	88	
Yachting	2,800	—	—	
Yachting, Model	200	—	—	

Notes

(a) The figures for whites were given by the Minister of Sport and Recreation in the South African Parliament on 25 March 1980. He stated that the numbers had been supplied by the 'national sports controlling bodies'.[1]

(b) The figures for Africans were provided by the Minister for Co-operation and Development on 26 February 1980. He did not explain their source.[2]

(c) The figures for Coloureds were given by the Minister of Coloured Relations on 26 February 1980. He stated that 'the promotion of sports for Coloured persons in the Republic by granting funds for the purchase of equipment and defraying of administrative expenses is a matter falling under the control of the Coloured Persons Representative Council and administered country-wide by its executive.' He stated that he had, however, ascertained that the answers to the question are as follows in so far as the Administration of Coloured Affairs is concerned'.[3]

(d) For Indians, the Minister of Indian Affairs stated in a reply to a request for estimates of the numbers actively participating in various sports that 'statistics in this regard are not available'.[4]

(e) Referred to as Horse Riding.

(f) Combined figures for Weightlifting and Body Building.

During 1981, the Minister of National Education was asked for estimates of the numbers of Coloured persons, excluding school children, who actively participated in each kind of sport. He replied that 'separate numbers are not available for the various population groups. The following numbers have been furnished by the national controlling bodies in respect of each kind of sport'.[5] He proceeded to cite figures for a total of 99 different sports. Almost identical figures were given, this time for a total of 104 sports, by the same Minister in February 1982.[6] The national controlling bodies cited by the Minister work within the framework of the South African government policy. These figures, therefore, did not include persons who pursue their activities through the various anti-apartheid sports bodies such as the South African Council on Sport.

In February 1982, the Minister of Co-operation and Development gave the following figures for the 'estimated number of Black (African) persons, excluding school children who actively participated in each kind of sport'.[7]

Athletics 16,144
Badminton 126
Body Building 1,714
Bowls 186
Bowling 12,499
Chess 744
Cricket 3,831
Cycling 156
Dancing 1,564
Darts 280
Dominoes 675
Draughts 100
Fresh Water Fishing 20
Golf 4,957
Gymnastics 1,732
Karate/Judo 6,779
Marathon 649
Netball/Basketball 11,158
Rugby 17,980
Snooker 50
Soccer (Football) 400,000
Softball 4,301
Squash 35
Swimming 3,262
Table Tennis 2,760

References and Abbreviations

The following abbreviations are used:

CH	–	*Cape Herald*
Cit	–	*The Citizen*, Johannesburg
CT	–	*Cape Times*
DD	–	*Daily Dispatch*, East London
FM	–	*Financial Mail*, Johannesburg
GN	–	*The Guardian*, London
NM	–	*Natal Mercury*, Durban
Obs	–	*Observer*, London
Post	–	*Post*, Johannesburg
RDM	–	*Rand Daily Mail*, Johannesburg
S.Exp	–	*Sunday Express*, Johannesburg
ST	–	*Sunday Times*, Johannesburg
Star	–	*Star*, (weekly airmail edition) Johannesburg
T	–	*The Times*, London
Tel	–	*Daily Telegraph*, London

Introduction
1. B J Vorster, Prime Minister, Parliamentary Debate on Sport, *Debates* 23.4.71.
2. *Sunday Tribune*, Dublin, 29.3.81.

1. History—Internal Resistance
1. Pamphlet published by the non-racial South African Amateur Swimming Federation, January 1974.
2. Memorandum submitted by SACOS to the International Tennis Federation, February 1978.

2. The Legal Basis of Apartheid Sport
1. Muriel Horrell, *Laws Affecting Race Relations in South Africa 1948-1976* (South African Institute of Race Relations 1978).
2. Horrell, *op.cit.*
3. *Ibid.*
4. *Star* 10.9.77.
5. *RDM* 25.8.77.

3. Repression
1. *Debates* 31.3.78.
2. *Debates* 6.2.80
3. *RDM* 13.12.81.

4. *RDM* 14.2.81.
5. *Cit* 8.7.81.
6. *T* 8.10.81.
7. *ST* 25.1.81.
8. *Cit* 11.11.81.
9. *CH* 10.10.81.
10. *DD* 4.9.81.
11. *Debates* 28.8.81.
12. Memorandum from Sylvia Coles to SAN-ROC, 29 October 1979.

5. Accomplices of the State
1. *Star* 28.5.62.
2. Booklet on 'community councils', published by the South African Department of Information, 1978.
3. P J Koornhof, Minister of Sport and Recreation, *Debates* 4.6.76.
4. P J Koornhof, Minister of Sport and Recreation, *Debates* 18.5.77.
5. *Sunday Tribune*, Dublin, 29.3.81.

5. Manoeuvres to Break Out of Isolation
1. P J Koornhof, Minister of Sport and Recreation, Parliamentary Debate on Sport, *Debates* 18.5.77.
2. *Ibid.*

3. Excerpt of a letter to a black sports administrator from Secretary of Sport and Recreation, 22 October 1976.
4. Excerpt of a letter to a black sports club from Secretary of Sport and Recreation, 3 December 1976.
5. *Debates* 21.5.79.
6. See Document VII.
7. Minister of Sport and Recreation, Parliamentary Debate on Sport, *Debates* 21.5.79.
8. *ST* 1.11.81.
9. *CH* 21.11.81.
10. *CH* 29.5.82.
11. *CH* 14.11.81.
12. Muriel Horrell, *Laws Affecting Race Relations in South Africa 1948-1976* (South African Institute of Race Relations 1978); and see Chapter II.
13. Muriel Horrell, *op.cit.*
14. *Sport in South Africa,* Report of the British Sports Council's fact-finding delegation, January 1980.
15. Minister of Industries, Commerce and Tourism, *Debates* 14.8.81.
16. *RDM* 25.3.82.
17. Memorandum presented to the South African Parliament, September 1980, paras. 1.8 and 1.9; see Document VIII.
18. *Star* 22.8.81.
19. *Ibid.*
20. D J de Villiers, Minister of Industries, Commerce and Tourism, *Debates* 2.10.81.
21. S A Pitman, *Debates* 17.3.82.
22. S F Kotze, Minister of Community Development, *Debates* 17.3.82.
23. *Ibid;* and see Document II.
24. K D S Durr, *Debates* 22.3.82.
25. D J Dalling, *Debates* 2.10.81.
26. *Debates* 16.3.82.
27. *Debates* 2.10.81.

6. International Missions
1. Letter dated 24 October 1980 from the South African Consul-General in London.
2. Letter from Paul Stephenson to P W Botha, 15 September 1980.
3. *Debates* 21.5.79.
4. *Sunday Times,* London, 4.5.80.
5. *NM* 13.3.80.
6. *GN* 4.6.80.
7. South African television broadcast, 6.6.79.

8. ITF Newsletter, 20.5.81.
9. Pamphlet issued by the South African National Olympic Committee in August 1980, which quoted the unofficial ICC delegation's report. The latter has never been made publicly available. The South African National Olympic Committee is a government-recognised and approved body, not to be confused with the South African Non-Racial Olympic Committee, SAN-ROC.
10. *Star* 25.4.80.

7. The Boycott Weapon
1. Report of the Secretary of Sport and Recreation for the calendar year 1978.
2. P J Badenhorst, Parliamentary Debate on Sport, *Debates* 22.5.80.
3. *Washington Post* 16.8.81.
4. *Boston Globe* 23.9.81.
5. *Daily Mirror,* London, 2.3.82.
6. *Daily Express,* London, 2.3.82.
7. *Daily Mail,* London, 2.3.82.
8. *The Standard,* London, 13.7.82.
9. *Daily Mirror,* London, 12.7.82.
10. *The Sun* London, 14.7.82.
11. *GN* 12.7.82.
12. *Daily Mail,* London, 13.7.82.
13. *Ibid.*
14. *Tel* 14.7.82.
15. *RDM* 22.9.81.
16. *CT* 7.12.81.
17. *Obs* 28.6.81.

8. Sponsorship
1. *RDM* 25.5.82.
2. *RDM* 25.3.82.
3. *S.Exp* 4.7.82.
4. *S.Exp* 28.2.82.
5. South African House of Assembly, Debates of the Standing Committee 2-82.
6. *Debates* 8.2.82.
7. *South African Digest* 16.3.79.
8. *RDM* 6.4.78.
9. *Sunday Tribune,* Durban, *Herald* (township supplement) 11.4.82.
10. *CH* 27.5.82.
11. *Ibid.*
12. *Daily Mail,* London, 12.7.82.
13. *GN* 2.3.82.
14. *Daily Mirror,* London, 12.7.82.
15. *Star* 23/27.2.80.
16. Chairman's Statement, 19 May 1981.
17. *RDM* 2.10.80.

18. *ST* 10.1.82.
19. *S.Exp* 30.3.80.
20. *RDM* 18.6.82.
21. *South African Digest* 16.3.79; *FM* 26.8.77, 24.3.78.
22. *Star* 11.12.81.
23. *RDM* 11.9.80.
24. *Star* 8.1.81.
25. *Star* 12.7.80.
26. *Star* 2.8.80.
27. *Post* 30.6.78.
28. *South African Digest* 16.3.79; *FM* 26.8.77, 24.3.78.
29. *RDM* 21.4.82.
30. *RDM* 23.2.80; *FM* 24.3.78.
31. *RDM* 13.12.81.
32. *RDM* 25.9.81.
33. *S.Exp* 29.11.81.
34. *South African Digest* 16.3.79; *FM* 26.8.77, 24.3.78.
35. *RDM* 18.12.81.
36. *Star* 5.12.80.
37. *RDM* 9.9.80.
38. *Star* 2.8.80.
39. *ST* 30.8.81.
40. *RDM* 19.3.82.
41. *Star* 27.2.80.
42. *ST* 29.7.81.
43. *Star* 8.1.81.
44. *Cit* 17.6.82.
45. *Cit* 29.5.80.
46. *South African Digest* 16.3.79; *FM* 26.8.77, 24.3.78.
47. *Sunday Tribune,* Durban, 19.7.81.
48. *Cit* 6.7.82.
49. *Cit* 26.6.82.
50. *Star* 23.2.80.

9. The United Nations Register of Sports Contacts with South Africa
1. United Nations Centre against Apartheid, Press Release No. 53/80, 24 October 1980.

. Conclusion
1. *Cit* 20.3.82.

. Appendix I
1. *Debates* 2.4.82.
2. *Debates* 25.3.80.
3. *Debates* 26.2.81.

. Appendix II
1. *Debates* 25.3.80.

. Appendix III
1. *Debates* 25.3.80.
2. *Debates* 26.2.80.
3. *Ibid.*
4. *Debates* 7.2.80.
5. *Debates* 13.8.81.
6. *Debates* 8.2.82.
7. *Debates* 22.2.82.